# SEATTLE

## TRAVEL GUIDE
## 2023

*The Ultimate Guide To Seattle For First Time visitors; Uncover The Hidden Gems, Must-See- Site, Top Attractions, Cuisines, Activities, Best Places & Nightlife*

**Winifred M. Cleveland**

# Table Of Contents

# INTRODUCTION

Welcome to Seattle, the Pacific Northwest's Emerald City! Seattle is a bustling and varied city that provides something for everyone. It is located between the seas of Puget Sound and the snow-capped summits of the Cascade Mountains. You'll find enough to keep you occupied in Seattle, whether you want to explore the city's outdoor attractions, enjoy its bustling cultural scene, or sample the numerous tastes of its world-class restaurants.

The city's scenery is as varied as its inhabitants. Seattle has something for everyone, from the busy downtown centre to the picturesque grandeur of the surroundings and lakes. Seattle has it all, whether you're searching for a weekend of shopping and sightseeing or a week of outdoor activity.

The city also has a plethora of entertainment options. There are several sites to see, ranging from the renowned Space Needle to the Seattle Aquarium. There is also a strong art culture in the city, with galleries, museums, and theatres displaying the work of local and foreign artists. Not to mention the Seattle music scene, which has produced some of the world's most famous performers.

Seattle is ideal for a laid-back weekend of discovery or an action-packed excursion. Come explore the city's distinct culture and history, and let your Seattle journey begin.

## My First Time Visit To Seattle

I had always wanted to visit Seattle, so when the opportunity presented itself, I seized it.I arrived in Seattle on a lovely day, and the city was humming with activity. Everything seemed so colourful and alive, and I knew I was in for a fantastic trip. The first thing I did was go on a tour of the city. The famous Space Needle was the first item that drew my attention. It seemed to be the city's focal point and a sign of its distinct character. I couldn't help but snap a few shots since I was so happy to be there.
I decided to go exploring and ended up at Pike Place Market. I was astounded by the variety of fresh fruit and seafood available, and I even stopped to listen to the street entertainers. I saw the iconic Space Needle, the lovely waterfront, and the many interesting shops and restaurants too.At a local cafe, I tried my first Seattle-style coffee and was pleasantly surprised by the rich and robust flavour. I was in awe of the city and everything it had to offer.

Following my trip, I decided to visit some of the surrounding communities. I strolled around Capitol Hill, Belltown, and Fremont, soaking in the sights and noises. I stopped in some of the local shops and spoke with some of the friendly locals. Everyone was kind and willing to offer tales and tips.

Then I went to some of the city's most popular attractions. I ascended to the top of the Space Needle and marvelled at the amazing views of the city and neighbouring mountains. I also visited the Seattle Art Museum and the Museum of Pop Culture. Everywhere I went, I felt like I was a part of living history.

I decided to unwind at one of the numerous parks after a few hours of wandering. While resting on a seat in a peaceful spot, I was able to take in the wonderful views of the city. It was a genuinely wonderful experience to feel the tranquillity of the city wash over me.

As the trip ends, I realised I had only scratched the surface of Seattle. I knew I would have to return soon to explore the city more and enjoy all it has to offer.

# CHAPTER 1: SEATTLE OVERVIEW

## History of Seattle

Seattle, the biggest metropolis in the **Pacific Northwest,** has a long history dating back millennia. The city was founded by **Europeans** in **1851** by a group of immigrants headed by **Arthur A. Denny**, as the ancestral home of the **Duwamish** and **Suquamish tribes**.

The city was founded in **1865** and swiftly evolved to become a significant port and economic centre due to its proximity to the **Pacific Ocean**. By the early **1900s**, Seattle had grown into a major industrial town, with a strong lumber industry and a thriving fishing sector.

As the city prospered, it drew immigrants from all over the globe, including **Scandinavians**, **Asians**, and **African Americans**. This flood of people from many nationalities and backgrounds helped define Seattle's culture, which can still be observed today.

The aerospace sector helped the city undergo a significant economic boom in the **1950s** and **1960s**. Boeing and other large aerospace industries established themselves in the region, providing thousands of employment to Seattle and the surrounding area.

In the late **1960s** and early **1970s,** Seattle was renowned as the cradle of the grunge music movement, with bands such as **Nirvana** and **Pearl Jam** calling **the city home**. This earned Seattle a reputation as an artistic and cultural hub, and the city has since been recognized for its strong music scene, progressive morals, and dynamic art scene.

Seattle was the core of the tech boom in the late **1980s** and early **1990s**, with Microsoft, Amazon, and other computer businesses establishing offices there. This enhanced the city's status as a technological hub, and Seattle is today a significant centre for technology and innovation. Seattle has come a long way from its days as a modest port and timber town, and it is still evolving and growing. From its Native American origins to its varied culture and current tech economy, Seattle is a city with a rich past and a promising future.

# Geography and Climate

Geography: Seattle is the biggest city in the state of Washington and the 15th largest metropolitan area in the United States, located on Puget Sound in the Pacific Northwest. It is bounded to the east by the Cascade Mountains, to the west by the Olympic Mountains, to the northwest by the Kitsap Peninsula, and to the south by the Columbia River.

Seattle's geography is highly diversified, with rolling hills, steep ravines, and a number of tiny lakes. West Tiger Mountain, situated in the Cascade Range, is Seattle's highest point, rising to a height of 2,759 feet (842 m). Much of Seattle is built on hills, with the downtown core situated on a hill known as "First Hill." Lake Washington, the biggest lake in the state of Washington, cuts through the city to the north and south.

The city of Seattle is home to many important rivers, including the Duwamish, Green, and Cedar rivers. The Duwamish River runs through town and drains into Elliott Bay, while the Green and Cedar rivers also empty into Lake Washington. In addition, the city is situated on Puget Sound, a major entrance of the Pacific Ocean.

Seattle also features many microclimates. Summers in the city are hot and dry, with temperatures ranging from 60 to 80 degrees Fahrenheit (15-26 degrees Celsius). Winters are frequently chilly and rainy, with temperatures ranging from 30 to 50 degrees Fahrenheit (-1 to 10 degrees Celsius).

Overall, Seattle's landscape is highly varied and diversified, making it an interesting and one-of-a-kind city to explore.

**Climate:** Seattle is well-known for its pleasant, rainy winters and relatively warm, dry summers. The area is distinguished by chilly, damp winters and rather dry, bright summers. Rainfall is equally distributed throughout the year, with the wettest months being October through April. July and August are the driest months, however Seattle receives rain even in these months.

Because of its position in the Pacific Northwest, Seattle has a maritime climate, with temperatures tempered by the ocean and the Puget Sound. This implies that Seattle has pleasant temperatures throughout the year, seldom hitting extremes of cold or heat. The average temperature throughout the year is roughly 55°F (13°C).

In the winter, Seattle is often damp and moderate. The average high temperature in the winter months (December-February) ranges from 45°F (7°C) to 50°F (10°C). The coldest month of the year is generally January, when temperatures may dip to an average low of 36°F (2°C). Snow is uncommon in Seattle, with the area getting an average of 2-4 inches (5-10 cm) each year.

Summer days are often warm and dry. Summertime maximum temperatures vary from 65°F (18°C) to 70°F (21°C). The warmest month of the year is often August, when the average low temperature is about 55°F (13°C). During the summer, Seattle receives less than 1 inch (2.5 cm) of rain on average.

Though Seattle is known for its wet winters and dry summers, the region does experience other types of weather. Wind gusts of up to 60 mph (96.5 km/h) may be expected in Seattle on occasion. The area is also prone to earthquakes, but most are mild and inflict little to no harm.

Overall, the temperature in Seattle is temperate and pleasant, making it a fantastic area to live and visit. The region's temperate temperatures, limited snowfall, and abundant sunlight make it an appealing location for both outdoor sports and sightseeing.

# Culture and People

**Culture:** Seattle's culture is dynamic, diversified, and frequently defined by its diverse population and strong arts scene. Seattle is home to several cultural institutions and organisations, including the **Seattle Art Museum, the Seattle Symphony, the Seattle Opera, and the Pacific Northwest Ballet.** Furthermore, Seattle is well-known for its specialty coffee shops, craft breweries, and thriving music scene.

Seattle is known as the Emerald City because of its beautiful green terrain and location on the Puget Sound. The city is home to a diverse spectrum of nationalities and cultures, including **Chinese, Japanese, Korean, Vietnamese,** and **Filipinos.** This diversity is mirrored in the city's food, which offers a wide range of Asian specialties. Seattle is also well-known for its seafood, with restaurants serving fresh fish from the adjacent Puget Sound.

The city is host to a variety of well-known events, including Bumbershoot, the Seattle International Film Festival, and the Bite of Seattle. The Seattle Center houses the Museum of Pop Culture, the Pacific Science Center, and the Seattle Opera House. Furthermore, the city has an impressive collection of art galleries, theatres, and music venues.

The city's lively culture, diversified people, and various attractions make it an appealing destination for tourists. Seattle is an excellent location for discovering and experiencing Pacific Northwest culture and traditions.

**Population:** Seattle's population is varied and energetic, influenced by the city's distinctive history, geography, and culture. With a population of approximately **750,000** people, the city is home to a diverse range of ethnic groups, including **African Americans and Asians.** Native Americans were the first people to settle in the Seattle region thousands of years ago. The first European settlers came in the mid-nineteenth century and founded Seattle. The city thrived and prospered swiftly, becoming an important port city in the Pacific Northwest.Seattle's population today is a melting pot of many distinct ethnicities. The city has a sizable African American, Asian, Pacific Islander, and Latino population. These groups are well-represented in municipal politics, business, and culture.
Seattle's population is both dynamic and diversified. They construct a distinct and great city by drawing on their own history, geography, and culture.

**People:** Seattle residents are also noted for their distinct fashion sense. Seattle is known for its grunge music culture, and its residents often wear plaid shirts, trousers, and hoodies. Seattle is also well-known for its technology sector, and many residents work in it or have launched their own tech enterprises.

Seattle residents are also recognized for their love of the outdoors. The city is surrounded by mountains, woods, and lakes, and its residents love outdoor activities like camping, hiking, and kayaking. There is also a vibrant music culture in the city, with several live music venues, festivals, and concerts.

## Language in Seattle

Seattle is a melting pot of languages and cultures. Many different native communities call Seattle home, and the languages spoken there reflect this diversity.

**English**, the city's official language, is the most widely spoken language in Seattle. English is the predominant language of more than 60% of the population. **Spanish, Chinese, Vietnamese, Tagalog, Korean, German, Russian, and French** are among the various languages spoken in Seattle.

The Duwamish and Suquamish tribes, as well as the Native American communities of Seattle, have their own languages, **Lushootseed** and *Suquamish*. These languages are taught in language classes and programs throughout the city by a small but dedicated community of native speakers.

Seattle also boasts a thriving African American community with its own language and culture. **African American Vernacular English (AAVE),** a dialect of English spoken by African Americans in the United States, is included.

Seattle's immigrant population is likewise quite varied, and many of these immigrants bring their own languages with them. The most widespread of these languages is *Spanish*, which is spoken by more than 20% of the population.

## Etiquette in Seattle

Seattle is a dynamic and varied city with a distinct culture and manners that reflect its rich past. Seattle offers something for everyone, from its vibrant culinary and cultural sectors to its different neighbourhoods and outdoor activities. While the city is known for its relaxed atmosphere and friendly locals, there are a few etiquette guidelines to follow. Understanding

Seattle etiquette may help you make the most of your stay in the Emerald City, from honouring local traditions and tipping generously to avoiding chatting too loudly on public transit.

## Greetings

A warm and courteous approach characterises Seattle greeting etiquette. When meeting someone for the first time, handshakes are the most popular way to welcome them. Eye contact and a smile are both essential components of a great introduction. Also when meeting someone in Seattle, it is necessary to address them nicely and by their name. It is also necessary to listen carefully and answer wisely.

When attending social or business functions, it is important to greet each person separately. A genuine and kind smile is always welcomed. Try to make small chat, even if it is short. This is a terrific approach to start a relationship.

When leaving a gathering, it is customary to say goodbye to each person individually. In Seattle, a handshake is the proper way to bid farewell.

When it comes to greeting etiquette in Seattle, it is essential to be aware of the cultural variations. Native Americans, African Americans, and other minority groups may have their own customary greeting. When greeting someone, it's crucial to show respect and consider their cultural background.

In general, greeting etiquette in Seattle is comparable to that of most other cities in the United States. When meeting someone new, it's crucial to be courteous, smile, and create eye contact. It is equally crucial to be aware of and appreciate cultural differences.

As a guest, you should observe the same decorum as the residents.

## Customs and Traditions

Seattle is a dynamic and varied city with a rich cultural heritage. Seattle's customs and traditions are firmly ingrained in its past and reflect the city's distinct identity.

*Tipping* is a well-known habit in Seattle. It is a significant element of Seattle culture and is required while eating out or getting services. The usual charge is 15-20% of the overall cost. When visiting Seattle, it is critical to be aware of the cultural norms, as tipping is an important part of the service industry.

Seattle is famed for its **coffee culture**, and the city has some of the top coffee shops in the world. Another Seattle custom is 'latte art,' which includes making patterns in the froth of a cappuccino or latte. This is a highly valued ability in Seattle, and it is an excellent way to impress locals.

Seattle is a city full of festivals and festivities. **The Seattle Seafair,** a ten-day summer celebration, is one of the most well-known. This event honours Seattle's marine history with parades, air shows, and other festivities.

It is critical to respect the environment in Seattle. There is a great focus on **recycling and eliminating trash,** and it is vital to keep this in mind while visiting the city.

Seattle is an outdoor-oriented city, and many of the local traditions focus around outside activities. Hiking and camping are popular activities, and it is essential to be aware of the *local fauna* and to preserve the environment.

The people of Seattle are kind and inviting, and it is crucial to respect their customs and traditions. If in doubt, it is always best to seek advice from locals before engaging in any activities.

## Dress Code

In Seattle, the clothing code is extremely loose and informal. Because the city is known for its laid-back atmosphere and casual style, it's important to dress appropriately.

**Business casual** is the most acceptable attire for the workplace. A collared shirt, dress trousers or khakis(jeans), decent shoes, and a belt are typical. A blazer or sport coat is not required. It is also fine for ladies to wear a skirt or dress that is not too exposing.

It's vital to dress up a little while going out in the evening. A good dress or top and pants, as well as stylish shoes and accessories, are ideal. It's also critical that you don't divulge too much.

When going out during the day, it's best to dress casually. Jeans, T-shirts, and shoes are all appropriate attire. In other regions, shorts and flip-flops are also appropriate.

It is important to dress correctly for formal occasions. This generally entails males wearing a suit or tuxedo and ladies wearing a lovely dress.

Overall, Seattle's dress code etiquette is extremely loose and informal. When selecting an outfit, it is critical to consider the occasion as well as the location. You should be fine as long as you're not too exposed and look presentable.

# CHAPTER 2: PLANNING AHEAD FOR SEATTLE TRIP

A well-planned vacation to Seattle is vital. There are many things to think about before visiting the city, whether for business or pleasure. Taking the time to prepare ahead can ensure that you get the most out of your vacation, from booking flights and accommodations to preparing a budget and researching activities. In this article, we'll go over how to plan your Seattle trip, such as where to stay and eat, activities, and more. With proper planning, you can ensure that your vacation to Seattle is fun and memorable.

## Budgeting & Money

Planning a vacation to Seattle may be a thrilling adventure, particularly if you are on a tight budget. There are several ways to conserve money while still enjoying yourself in the Emerald City. Here is some money-management and budgeting advice for your vacation to Seattle.

**First,** plan ahead of time and conduct research. Look up typical rates for nearby attractions, hotels, and restaurants. This will assist you in creating a realistic budget and controlling your expenditures. Also, book your flights, hotels, and attractions ahead of time to get the best deals.

**Second,** seek free things to do in the city. Exploring Pike Place Market, wandering through the Seattle Art Museum, and seeing the Hiram M. Chittenden Locks are all free activities to do in Seattle. Many of the city's parks, beaches, and trails are also open to the public.

**Third,** try eating at lesser-known establishments. Many of Seattle's restaurants are known for charging exorbitant prices, but there are also plenty of low-cost options. To save money, look for food trucks, local pubs, and off-the-beaten-path places. Additionally, look for coupons and discounts for nearby restaurants.

**Fourth,** make use of public transit. Buses, light rail, and ferries are part of the city's large public transit system. This is a terrific way to save money on transportation while still having fun seeing the city.

**Finally,** always budget for unanticipated costs. It's a good idea to have some extra cash on hand in case anything unexpected happens. This will help you stay inside your budget and avoid spending more than you can afford.

You may have a lovely vacation to Seattle while remaining within your budget if you follow these recommendations. Have a fantastic day discovering the Emerald City!

# Visas & Immigration

## VISA

If you want to visit Seattle, Washington, you will need to get a U.S. visa before entering the country. The visa procedure might be long and difficult depending on the purpose of your travel and the nation you originate from. Here's everything you need to know and do to receive your Seattle visa.

### Step 1: Determine Your Visa Type
The first step in obtaining a visa to Seattle is determining what sort of visa you will need. Depending on the purpose of your visit, several visas are available. It is possible to get a business visa, a student visa, a tourist visa, or a work visa.

### Step 2: Obtain the Documentation Required
After determining the kind of visa you need, you must obtain the relevant papers. A valid passport, a completed visa application, a

passport-sized picture, and any other papers needed by the visa type are all necessary.

## Step 3: Pay Your Fees
You must pay the necessary visa costs. These differ depending on the visa type and the country of origin.

### Student Visa
The cost of a student visa to Seattle varies based on the kind of visa you are seeking for. If you are applying for an F-1 student visa, you must pay an application cost of $160, a SEVIS I-901 charge of $200, and a visa issuance fee of $275. If you are applying from outside the United States, you may be required to pay extra expenses such as a courier charge.

### Visa for Work:
The cost of a work visa to Seattle is determined on the kind of visa requested. If you apply for an H-1B visa, you must pay the filing charge of $460, the American Competitiveness and Workforce Improvement Act of 1998 **(ACWIA)** fee of $750 or $1,500, the Fraud Prevention and Detection charge of $500, and the visa issue fee of $275. If you are applying from outside the United States, you

may be required to pay extra expenses such as a courier charge.

## Business Visa

The cost of a business visa to Seattle is determined on the kind of visa applied for. If you are applying for a B-1 visa, you must pay an application cost of $160 as well as a visa issuance fee of $275. If you are applying from outside the United States, you may be required to pay extra expenses such as a courier charge.

## Tourist visa:

The cost of a tourist visa to Seattle is determined on the kind of visa applied for. If you are applying for a B-2 visa, you must pay an application cost of $160 as well as a visa issuance charge of $275. If you are applying from outside the United States, you may be required to pay extra expenses such as a courier charge.

## Step 4: Complete and Submit Your Application

You must submit your visa application to the nearest US embassy or consulate. Make sure to include all required documentation and to follow the instructions.

### Step 5: Arrange an Interview

If your visa application is approved, you must schedule an interview at the nearest United States embassy or consulate. During the interview, you will be asked about your history, purpose of trip, and financial situation.

### Step 6: Await Results

You must wait for the outcome of your visa application. A decision may take many weeks or months to be made.

You will be allowed to enter the United States after you have gotten your visa. Have a wonderful time in Seattle!

# Money and Currency

The US Dollar (USD) is the currency used in Seattle. Seattle is the biggest city in the state of Washington and an important hub of trade, industry, and culture in the Pacific Northwest area. As a result, it is home to a number of financial institutions, as well as several companies and people that trade in both local and foreign currencies.However, other popular currencies are also accepted. This includes the Canadian Dollar (CAD), Euro (EUR), Japanese Yen (JPY), British Pound (GBP), and Swiss

Franc (CHF). There are also a variety of foreign exchange kiosks and money changers in the city, enabling tourists and locals to transfer their currencies into US dollars.

In addition to currency exchange, Seattle boasts a thriving financial industry. Banks such as Bank of America, Wells Fargo, and Chase provide a variety of services such as checking and savings accounts, mortgages, and credit cards. There are also many smaller, regionally owned banks that may offer more specialised services.

There are several ways to spend money in Seattle. Cash is accepted everywhere, although debit and credit cards are also extensively used. Furthermore, visitors from other countries can shop in their home currency. There are additional ATMs located across the city that enable guests to withdraw cash in USD.

Finally, the Seattle area is home to numerous financial services and technology firms, making it a financial innovation hotspot. Companies located in Seattle include Amazon and Microsoft, which provide a wide range of financial services to its consumers. As a consequence, Seattle is an excellent destination to invest since it provides both local and worldwide prospects.

# Time Difference

One of the most crucial things to remember for first-time visitors to Seattle is the time difference. Seattle is in the Pacific Time Zone, which is 8 hours behind Coordinated Universal Time (UTC). This implies that at 12:00 UTC, it is only 4:00 a.m. in Seattle.

The time difference between Seattle and other locations across the globe may be rather large. The time difference between Seattle and New York City, for example, is 3 hours, whereas the time difference between Seattle and London is 8 hours.

Daylight Saving Time (DST) is observed in Seattle, however the precise dates vary year to year. During DST, clocks in Seattle advance by one hour, reducing the time difference between Seattle and other cities by one hour. For example, during DST, the time difference between Seattle and London is 7 hours.

When travelling to Seattle from another country, it is critical to keep these time differences in mind. For example, if you want to phone a friend or family member in Seattle from New York, you must call at least 3 hours sooner than you would ordinarily call in New York.

It's also worth noting that the time difference between Seattle and other locations may change substantially depending on the season. For example, during the summer, the time difference between Seattle and New York is just 2 hours, however in the winter, it may be as much as 4 hours.

Visitors visiting Seattle may ensure that all of their appointments, meetings, and calls are arranged at the right time by knowing the time difference between Seattle and other cities.

## Packing Tips

If you're considering a vacation to Seattle, Washington, make sure you're prepared for the weather and activities the city has to offer. There's lots to do, from exploring the city's burgeoning music and cultural scene to admiring its breathtaking natural beauty. To make the most of your vacation, bring the essentials. This Seattle packing list will help you ensure that you have everything you need to enjoy the Emerald City.

1. Bring layers of clothes. Because Seattle is known for its unpredictable weather, bring layers of clothing. Pack light jackets, sweaters,

and rain gear such as a raincoat, umbrella, and waterproof shoes.

**2.** Bring comfortable shoes. Because Seattle is a walkable city, bring comfortable walking shoes.

**3.** Bring a reusable water bottle. Seattle offers lots of public drinking fountains and water bottle refills, so avoid the plastic and bring your own.

**4.** Bring a light raincoat. Even if it isn't raining when you arrive, you should bring a raincoat in case the weather changes.

**5.** Don't forget to bring an umbrella. If you are caught in a rainstorm, a decent quality umbrella will keep you dry.

**6.** Pack sunscreen and sunglasses. Don't forget to bring these basics with you to Seattle.

**7.** Bring a rain poncho. These are ideal for staying dry during light showers.

**8.** Pack a couple sweatshirts. It can be cold in Seattle, so pack a couple sweaters.

**9.** Bring a cap and gloves. Even in the summer, it may be chilly and windy in Seattle, so bring a hat and gloves.

**10.** Pack an extra bag. Bring an additional tote or backpack for keepsakes.

## Travel Insurance

Travelling to Seattle may be a joyful and exciting experience, but it is critical to ensure that you are adequately protected in the event of an emergency. Travel insurance can provide you with peace of mind and assist in covering unforeseen travel expenditures. Before travelling to Seattle, make sure to weigh all of your options for purchasing travel insurance.

Consider what sort of coverage you require before purchasing travel insurance. Medical bills, trip cancellation, lost or stolen luggage, and other unforeseen costs associated with travel are often covered by travel insurance. It may also include medical evacuation, emergency medical treatment, flying accident coverage, and automobile rental coverage, depending on the type of insurance you choose.

Compare multiple companies when shopping for travel insurance to discover the best coverage for your trip. Make sure to read the fine print and understand what is and is not covered. It's also worth noting that some policies may exclude particular activities, such as skiing, so read the tiny print carefully.

When looking for travel insurance in Seattle, keep the local laws and regulations in mind. When it comes to travel insurance, various states have different rules, so make sure you understand the laws in Seattle before getting coverage.

Finally, make sure you have travel insurance before you leave on your trip. Some travel insurance policies require you to buy the policy at least two weeks before your trip, so read the fine print carefully.

# When to Visit Seattle

## Best Time of Year

From late spring to early autumn is the finest time to visit Seattle. The weather is normally warm throughout this time, with temperatures ranging from the mid-50s to the mid-70s Fahrenheit. Summertime in Seattle means long days with lots of sunlight, making it a great time to explore the city.

Summer months are also the most popular for visitors due to the abundance of sights and activities. The Seattle Space Needle is open all year and offers excellent views of the city throughout the warmer months. Other popular summer attractions include the Seattle Aquarium, the Seattle Art Museum, and the Woodland Park Zoo. During the summer, the Pacific Science Center and the Seattle Great Wheel are also popular attractions.

The autumn season provides colder temperatures ranging from the mid-40s to the mid-60s Fahrenheit. This is an excellent time to get outside, as the crisp air and changing leaves make for an ideal hiking or camping trip. Hiking routes may be located all across town and are suitable for both beginner and expert hikers. The Seattle Great Wheel, a renowned Ferris wheel, is also open until the end of the season.

Seattle's winters may be chilly and rainy, with temperatures ranging from the mid-30s to the mid-50s Fahrenheit. It's an excellent time to visit the city's indoor attractions, such as the Seattle Aquarium, the Seattle Art Museum, and the Pacific Science Center. The Seattle Great Wheel is open all year, offering views of the city from the famed Ferris wheel.

Seattle is a fantastic city to come at any time of year. Seattle is an ideal location for vacationers of all ages, thanks to its temperate weather and wealth of activities.

## Weather

Summer is the greatest season to visit Seattle, Washington. The city has temperate weather and lots of sunlight, with an average temperature of 68°F (20°C). There will be lots of pleasant, bright days from June until September. During this time, the city also receives less rain, making it an ideal time to explore the city.

The months of April, May, and October are also ideal for a vacation to Seattle. Temperatures are moderate, ranging from the mid-50s to the mid-60s (13-18°C), with lots of sunny days. Spring and October are also ideal periods to appreciate Seattle's distinct natural beauty, with blossoming flowers in the spring and vibrant leaves in the fall.

During the winter, temperatures in Seattle can drop below freezing, and the weather is frequently cloudy and rainy. Snow is conceivable, although it is quite unlikely. While there are plenty of things to do in Seattle during the winter, it is not the best time for outdoor activities.

Summer is often the greatest season to visit Seattle. Warm, bright days are expected, with lots of outdoor activities.

## Events

There is never a bad time to go to Seattle! However, when it comes to the best time to visit Seattle, it really depends on the type of experience you seek.

If you're seeking warm weather and outdoor activities, the summer months of June, July, and August provide the most comfortable temperatures, which typically range from the upper 50s to the low 70s. The city comes alive with events and activities throughout these months, making them perfect for tourism. The Fremont Solstice Parade and the Seattle International Film Festival are both prominent events in June, while the Fourth of July fireworks extravaganza at Gas Works Park takes place in July.

Winter is a fantastic season to visit Seattle if you don't mind the cooler weather. From December to February, the city's distinctive skyline is snow-covered, and there are lots of chances for winter sports like skiing and snowboarding. The Seattle Boat Show and the Seattle Chocolate Festival, both popular events for foodies, are also held throughout the winter months.

Spring and autumn are perfect for finding a balance between the weather and the events. Spring brings pleasant weather and abundance of blossoms, as well as the Seattle Cherry Blossom & Japanese Cultural Festival and the Bite of Seattle. In the autumn, you can enjoy the city's vibrant autumn foliage as well as events such as the Seattle International Beerfest and the Seattle International Film Festival.

Whatever time of year you visit, Seattle has something for everyone. You'll have a fantastic time whether you choose to explore the city's outdoor attractions or attend a festival

# CHAPTER 3: GETTING AROUND SEATTLE

Do you want to visit Seattle but don't know how to get around? Don't worry, Seattle is a fantastic city to visit and offers an abundance of transit alternatives to get you where you need to go. There are several methods to get about the city. In this chapter I, we'll look at the various modes of transportation accessible in Seattle and how to utilise them. So, whether you're a first-time visitor or a Seattle local, you'll be able to find the most convenient way to get around.

## Public Transportation

In Seattle, public transit is an essential element of daily life. Seattle has an extensive public transit infrastructure that provides easy access to many of the city's most popular attractions. From light rail and buses to ferries and taxis, Seattle's public transit choices cater to both commuters and tourists.

### Metro Bus

The Metro Bus in Seattle is a popular mode of public transit for commuters, tourists, and locals alike. It is a handy, cost-effective, and dependable mode of transportation in the city. Metro Bus has been a component of the King County Metro Transit system since 1973.

Metro Bus has a fleet of approximately 1,400 buses that serve over 220 destinations around the county. The system is separated into three service types: local, express, and night. Local routes serve numerous communities and destinations on a regular basis, while express routes serve big cities quickly and directly. Night service is provided on select routes, making it a more cost-effective option to taxis.

## Riders ticket

Riders may buy tickets and passes via Metro ticket vending machines, online, or at any of the city's Metro outlets. Metro bus tickets and passes are valid on all Metro bus routes, including local, express, and night service. Riders may pay with cash on the bus as well, although precise change is necessary.

Every Metro bus is wheelchair accessible and has bike racks. There is also free Wi-Fi and real-time arrival information on the buses. In addition, many lines in downtown Seattle and the University District provide free rides.

Metro buses are an essential element of Seattle's transportation system, offering quick and inexpensive access to a variety of popular attractions. Metro Bus makes it simple to go about the city with its extensive network of bus routes and flexible ticketing alternatives.

The Metro Bus is one of the most popular modes of public transit in Seattle, Washington. The King County Department of Transportation operates the Metro Bus system, which covers over 120 routes across the county. The system features a bus route network that connects to a number of locations, including downtown Seattle, the University of Washington, downtown Bellevue, and Sea-Tac Airport.

## Cost & Discount

The Metro Bus system provides an inexpensive and easy method to travel across Seattle and the surrounding region. A single Metro Bus journey costs $2.50 for adults and $1.50 for children, pensioners, and individuals with disabilities. A day admission costs $5.00 for adults and $2.50 for children, pensioners, and individuals with disabilities.

The Metro Bus system provides a number of tools to assist travellers navigate the city. The system includes a mobile app as well as a website that provides real-time arrival information and trip planning features. Riders may also get route maps and timetables from the Metro Bus website, as well as utilise the interactive trip planner to discover the shortest route from A to B.

The Metro Bus system also accepts a variety of payment methods, including cash, ORCA cards, and credit/debit cards. ORCA cards are reloadable cards that enable passengers to save cash and passes for convenient access. The ORCA cards are available for purchase online or at most retail locations that carry the ORCA emblem. For anybody seeking a cheap and easy method to travel about Seattle, the Metro Bus system is a great choice. The system makes it simple to navigate about the city, with a number of routes and payment alternatives.

# Link Light Rail Transport

## The System

The Link Light Rail is a public transportation system operated by Sound Transit in Seattle, Washington. The system operates between Seattle-Tacoma(Sea-Tac) International Airport and Angel Lake in Seattle's Rainier Valley district. It operates 16 stations in Seattle, Tukwila, SeaTac, and Kent. The Link Light Rail launched in July 2009 and has since been an important aspect in connecting people and communities in the greater Seattle region.

The Link Light Rail is a public transportation system serving Seattle and the surrounding region. The Link Light Rail system connects the University of Washington in Seattle to Sea-Tac Airport by nearly 22 miles of track, with additional stops along the route. Sound Transit operates the system, which is part of the regional transit network.The system transports around 100,000 people every day, making it the country's second busiest light rail system, behind only the San Francisco BART system.

Within the Seattle metropolitan area, the Link Light Rail provides a convenient, safe, and cost-effective mode of transportation. It provides regular service, with trains every 6 to 15 minutes during peak hours.The trains' maximum speed is 55 mph, however the average speed on the system is closer to 25 mph.The Link Light Rail is also an excellent option to avoid traffic and parking complications. It is also a vital mode of transportation for those with impairments and others who do not have access to a vehicle.

## Cost,Discount & payment mode

The Link Light Rail system is both inexpensive and convenient. The system charges a set amount of **$2.50** and includes **transfers** every journey, regardless of distance travelled. There are also monthly passes available for purchase at a reduced cost. In addition, the Link Light Rail system provides a number of amenities such as bike racks, wheelchair access, and real-time arrival information.

Fares are also reduced for elderly, minors, and low-income users.

## Free fare zones

There are also some free fare zones, such as downtown Seattle, Capitol Hill, and the University of Washington. Free price zones make it simpler for passengers to use the Link Light Rail without having to pay a charge.

## Where to go

The Link Light Rail system is an essential component of Seattle's public transit system. Many of the city's attractions and entertainment venues, such as the Seattle Center, the Space Needle, and Pike Place Market, are accessible from here. It also links individuals with major companies and educational institutions like the University of Washington and Seattle Pacific University. Furthermore, the Link Light Rail connects to recreational areas such as Alki Beach, Golden Gardens Park, and the Olympic Sculpture Park.

# Taxis and Ride-Share Transport

**Taxis** and ride-sharing services have grown in popularity in Seattle, Washington, owing to the convenience and cost savings they provide. Taxis have been around for decades, but the emergence of ride-sharing application has transformed the way people travel about the city. Taxis are an excellent alternative for folks who need to go about fast and conveniently since they are accessible 24 hours a day and can be found at taxi stops located around the city. Taxis are a dependable and safe mode of transportation, with prices depending on distance and time. Taxis are also an excellent choice for people seeking a more private mode of transportation. Taxis are a fantastic alternative for people searching for a more private mode of transportation since they are dependable and safe.

**Ride-sharing services**, on the other hand, are a more cheap choice for individuals who need to travel about quickly and easily. The simplicity of ride-sharing applications is also attractive to Seattle residents. Rather than flagging down a cab on the street, customers may order a trip with a few touches on their smartphone. The app will then link them to a driver and offer an approximate time of arrival. This makes it much simpler to organise and manage excursions, particularly for those unfamiliar with the area.

## Free Cost zones

In addition to taxis and ride-sharing options, Seattle has cost-free zones. The City of Seattle has designated these places to offer a safe and inexpensive form of transportation for persons who cannot afford to pay for a typical taxi or ride-sharing service. Finally, for people who cannot afford to pay for a regular taxi or ride-sharing service, Seattle has free zones that give a safe and economical way to move about the city.These places are often placed near public transit, like the bus stations which provide a cost-effective option for individuals searching for a way to go about.

## Cheap choice

Trip-hailing applications like Uber and Lyft enable customers to request a trip from their smartphone, which is then linked to a driver in the region. This service substantially decreases the time and expense of hailing a cab. Ride-hailing apps, such as UberPool and Lyft Line, typically provide more affordable options for larger groups of people, allowing multiple riders to share a ride and split the cost.

They provide a convenient and cost-effective alternative to conventional taxi services. Users may schedule trips in advance using these services, and rates are calculated depending on time and distance. Users of ride-sharing platforms may also follow their drivers and offer comments on their experiences.

### Cost & Discount

The cost of a taxi route in Seattle might vary based on the time of day and the distance travelled. In general, it will cost around $2.50 for the first mile and $2.50 for each additional mile. In contrast, a ride-sharing app may cost as low as $1.00 per mile.

## Rentals Transport

**For Car:** Renting a car in Seattle is a terrific way to get about without the trouble and cost of owning a car. Seattle provides something for everyone in terms of rental alternatives and usage techniques.

### Cost & Discount

The cost of a rental car in Seattle might vary based on the kind of vehicle you hire, the amount of time you need it, and other considerations. A small automobile will typically cost approximately $50 per day to rent, but an SUV or minivan would cost more than $100 per day. Furthermore, some rental companies may offer additional discounts or packages that make renting a car more affordable.

In addition to the cost of renting a vehicle, you may be charged extra costs such as fuel charges and taxes. Fuel costs vary based on the car you hire and the distance you go. You may also be forced to pay a local tax or additional costs to the rental vehicle provider

**For Bikes:** Seattle has a range of bike rental alternatives for individuals who prefer two-wheeled mobility. Bike rentals are available at Cascade Bicycle Studio and Recycled Cycles. Riders may pick between road, mountain, and electric bikes.

### Cost & Discount

If you don't have your own bike, rental fees start about $20 for a full day.Seattle also has various public transit alternatives for individuals looking for a more economical option. The Metro Transit bus system serves the whole city and is a handy method to get about. It also provides reduced rates for elders, students, and those with disabilities.

Seattle also has an extensive network of bike and pedestrian pathways. These walkways are an excellent way to navigate about town and see the sites.

## Ferries Transport

### The system and service

In Seattle, ferry transportation is a terrific way to get about, providing a unique and picturesque means of transportation. Ferries are a handy and cost-effective means to travel throughout Puget Sound, linking several of the area's main communities. With a wide range of routes and services available, it is simple to choose the ideal ferry for your requirements.With 22 boats and ten routes linking 20 ports of call in Puget Sound, the San Juan Islands, and the Canadian Gulf Islands.

**Washington State Ferries (WSF)** is the biggest ferry system in the United States and the third largest in the world. It is also  part of the Washington State Department of Transportation, WSF runs the most ferry routes in the United States and is the only public transportation system in the Puget Sound area that connects Seattle and the San Juan Islands directly and which can transport up to 2,500 people and 200 cars on each journey.

Other ferry systems in the Puget Sound area exist in addition to WSF. The King County Water Taxi provides a rapid and accessible connection between downtown Seattle and West Seattle on a regular basis. The Kitsap Transit Fast Ferry links Seattle to Bremerton and Kingston, while the Victoria Clipper provides fast service to Victoria, British Columbia.

## Cost & Discount

WSF also provides a number of discounts and packages that make ferry travel more inexpensive. Monthly passes are available for regular ferry users, as are discounted tickets for individuals who qualify for reduced costs, such as elderly and those with disabilities. WSF also provides unique packages, such as the Washington State Ferry Adventure Package, which enables riders to spend two days and one night seeing the San Juan Islands and Olympic Peninsula.

The cost of using a ferry is determined on the route, ticket type, and number of people and vehicles. A single passenger normally pays between $8 and $10, while a car with a driver costs between $11 and $15. Seniors and students are eligible for discounts, and a one-day ticket is offered for $17.Fares between Seattle and the San Juan Islands, for example, start at $7.50 for adults, $3.50 for seniors, and $3.00 for children. Fares vary from $3.50 to $5.25 for individuals going by foot or bicycle. Fares for those going by automobile will be higher, ranging from $14.90 for a car to $60.70 for a truck with three axles.

The boat is one of Seattle's most popular and convenient modes of transportation. It is a quick method to move from one place to another in the city and a terrific way to take in the breathtaking vistas of Puget Sound and the Olympic Mountains.

With over 23 million passengers each year, Seattle's ferry system is quite popular. It is an excellent mode of transportation that provides a unique and gorgeous experience. The boats provide a quiet and pleasurable voyage with plenty of opportunity to explore the scenery. The boat system is an essential aspect of the city's transportation network and remains a popular mode of transit for both inhabitants and tourists.

Whatever type of ferry you choose, you can be assured of a scenic and convenient way to explore the Puget Sound region. With a wide range of routes and services available, it is simple to choose the ideal ferry for your requirements.

## Walking Tours

Walking tours are one of the most popular methods of discovering a city. Walking tours allow you to learn about a city and its culture while also offering an inexpensive and handy method to travel about. Walking tours in Seattle are a terrific way to see the city and learn about its history and culture.

Depending on the trip and the location being visited, these excursions may last anywhere from a few hours to several days. Walking tours in Seattle may include visits to some of the city's most recognizable landmarks, such as the Space Needle and Pike Place Market, as well as more off-the-beaten-path attractions, such as the Fremont Troll and the Seattle Underground Tour.

### Cost & Discount

The cost of a walking tour in Seattle varies based on the trip and its duration. Walking tours typically cost $25 to $50, with discounts available for groups and students. Furthermore, some walking tours, such as the Seattle Underground Tour or the Fremont Troll

Tour, may charge additional fees for special attractions.

## Cost Free Zones

Walking excursions are very affordable, making them excellent for budget tourists. Walking tours are often provided for free or at a low fee. There are also several free walking tours in Seattle, such as the Uptown Walking Tour and the Seattle Art Museum Tour. These excursions allow tourists to discover the city without having to spend a lot of money.

In addition, Seattle has a number of free attractions. The Pike Place Market, a lively outdoor market with over 200 merchants and eateries, is one of Seattle's most popular free attractions. Visitors are welcome to explore the market and its varied attractions.

Walking tours are an excellent way to learn about Seattle and its culture. They provide a handy and cost-effective method to explore the city and learn about its history, landmarks, and culture. With so many tours to select from, Seattle is sure to have something for everyone.

It is one of the most popular modes of transportation in Seattle, providing visitors with a unique way to explore the city's sights and sounds. **Walking tours are often conducted by an expert** who may give information about the city's history, culture, and attractions.

# CHAPTER 4:
# ACCOMMODATION IN
# SEATTLE

Seattle, sometimes known as the Emerald metropolis, is a dynamic and varied metropolis located between Puget Sound and Lake Washington. Seattle is a terrific location for tourists searching for a memorable experience, with its busy downtown and plenty of activities. From lovely bed & breakfasts to magnificent hotels, Seattle provides a broad choice of lodgings to suit every budget and style.Accommodation in Seattle spans from low-cost motels to luxurious apartments and everything in between. Whether you're searching for a short-term or long-term stay, you'll find the ideal location to call home in the city.

## Hotels

From budget-friendly hotels to five-star luxury resorts, Seattle boasts a variety of lodgings to accommodate every tourist. Hotels in Seattle have a range of services like fitness centres, pools, and on-site restaurants. The Fairmont Olympic Hotel, The Westin Seattle, and The Edgewater are among the most popular hotels in Seattle.There are various hostels in Seattle's downtown centre for those on a tight budget. A bed in a shared dorm room costs $50-$75 a night, while a private room costs up to $150 per night. Other amenities available at some hostels include a shared kitchen and lounge area, as well as free Wi-Fi.

If you want something a little more upmarket, there are many mid-range hotels that provide decent lodging at a fair price. A normal room costs between $150 and $200 per night, and many of these hotels have facilities such as free Wi-Fi, a pool, and a fitness centre.

For those seeking something more opulent, Seattle offers a plethora of high-end hotels to select from. Prices vary from $200 to $400 per night, including facilities such as a spa, concierge, pool, and complimentary Wi-Fi.

There are various extended-stay hotels in Seattle for folks who need to remain for an extended period of time. A standard room costs $150-$250 per night, while a suite costs up to $400 per night. A kitchenette, free Wi-Fi, and a fitness centre are possible amenities.

Whatever type of lodging you seek, you will undoubtedly find something in Seattle that meets your requirements and budget. You'll be able to locate the right location to stay in Seattle, from hostels to luxury apartments.

# Vacation Rentals

Vacation rentals are an excellent choice for those seeking a more private and home-like experience. Vacation rentals in Seattle range from small apartments to multi-bedroom mansions. Vacasa, Airbnb, and HomeAway are among the most popular vacation rental sites in Seattle.

Vacation rentals in Seattle are an excellent choice for those wishing to experience the Emerald City. You'll discover the ideal rental in Seattle, from downtown lofts to waterfront cottages, to make your stay comfortable and memorable.

The price of a vacation rental in Seattle varies according to its size, location, and amenities. Downtown apartments normally cost between $150 and $300 per night, while seaside villas may cost between $500 and $1,000 per night. The cost of vacation rental homes is also affected by the duration of your stay and the season.

You can anticipate a few basic conveniences while renting a vacation property in Seattle. A fully supplied kitchen with cooking and eating supplies, new bedding, and access to a washing and dryer are among the amenities. The majority of rentals also have cable or satellite TV, Wi-Fi, and a private patio or balcony.

Depending on the location, some Seattle vacation rentals may also have extra facilities such as a hot tub, pool, or gaming room. Furthermore, many of these properties provide access to community amenities like a gym, pool, or tennis court.

When booking your Seattle vacation rental, make sure to inquire about the rules and regulations. Smoking, dogs, and noise levels may be prohibited in certain rentals. It's also a good idea to double-check the property's cancellation policy before making a reservation.

Seattle vacation rentals are a fantastic hotel choice for those who wish to experience the city in comfort and luxury. With a wide range of rental homes to choose from, you're sure to discover the ideal rental to make your time in Seattle pleasurable.

# Hostels

Hostels are among the many accommodation alternatives in Seattle. Hostels provide an economical, communal living experience that is ideal for budget tourists. The city boasts a number of hostels in several areas, each with its own set of facilities and services.

The Green Tortoise Hostel is situated in the centre of downtown Seattle. It offers shared and individual dormitory-style accommodations, as well as a restaurant and bar. There is also a games room, a fully equipped kitchen, and a nice lounge space at the hostel. Dormitory beds cost $30 per night, while private rooms cost $95 per night.

The Capitol Hill district is home to City Hostel Seattle. It offers dormitory-style lodging in shared and individual rooms, as well as a fully equipped kitchen and a comfortable living space. Dormitory beds start at $25 per night, while private rooms start at $75 per night.

The Seattle International Hostel is in the Queen Anne area of Seattle. It offers shared and private rooms in a dormitory-style setting, as well as a community kitchen and a comfortable sitting space. Dormitory beds start at $30 per night, while private rooms start at $90 per night.

The Seattle Pacific Hostel is in the Fremont area of Seattle. It offers dormitory-style lodging in shared and individual rooms, as well as a fully equipped kitchen and a comfortable living space. Dormitory beds start at $25 per night, while private rooms start at $75 per night.

The University District is where you'll find Seattle U-District Hostel. It offers dormitory-style lodging in shared and individual rooms, as well as a fully equipped kitchen and a comfortable living space. Dormitory beds start at $30 per night, while private rooms start at $90 per night.

A hostel is the ideal housing choice for anybody seeking a cheap place to stay in Seattle or a community living experience. With a wide range of hostels spread across the city, you're likely to find one that meets your budget and requirements.

# Campgrounds

Seattle offers a fantastic assortment of campsites, offering a diverse range of possibilities for people seeking a unique and economical overnight option. Campgrounds in Seattle provide a range of locations and services to suit all sorts of tourists, from the rough coasts of the Olympic Peninsula to the calm woods of the Cascade Mountains.

The price of camping in Seattle varies substantially based on location, facilities, and season. Campgrounds typically charge between $20 to $50 a night, with some bigger campgrounds and RV parks charging weekly or monthly prices. Many campgrounds also give seniors, active military personnel, and AAA members discounts.

Campers have a range of camping options, including rustic sites, RV sites, and cabin rentals. Primitive camping is the cheapest choice, but it is also the most rudimentary, since there is no running water or power. RV sites are the most popular camping choice in Seattle, with full hookups and a range of amenities such as picnic tables and fire rings. Cabin rentals are also available, offering a secluded and pleasant stay with a fully equipped kitchen and bathroom.

Whatever type of camping experience you seek, Seattle has a campground for you. Showers, laundry facilities, Wi-Fi, and even swimming pools are available at many of the campsites in the region. Fishing, motorcycling, and hiking are just a few of the activities available at certain campsites.

When it comes to camping in Seattle, the options are almost limitless. There's something for every budget and lifestyle, whether you're searching for a rustic campground or a fully-equipped RV park. From the gorgeous Olympic Mountains to the rough Puget Sound shoreline, Seattle offers something for everyone!

# Bed and Breakfasts

Bed & breakfast hotel is an excellent choice for individuals seeking a unique and customised experience when visiting Seattle. Bed & breakfasts, as opposed to standard hotels, offer a more private and homely setting with customised service. Many bed and breakfasts in Seattle offer stunning views of the waterfront, mountains, and city skyline, creating a picturesque setting that enhances the experience.

The cost of a bed and breakfast stay in Seattle may vary substantially based on the location and services provided. A single night in a basic accommodation will typically cost between $100 and $200. If you want anything more upscale, expect to spend between $200 and $400 each night.

Most Seattle bed and breakfasts provide a variety of facilities regardless of price. These include complimentary breakfast, free Wi-Fi, and on-site parking. Most bed & breakfasts also provide comfortable, warm rooms with private bathrooms, flat-screen TVs, and other amenities. Some bed & breakfasts also give access to a common kitchen and sitting room, allowing visitors to meet and mix with other tourists.

When it comes to activities, most bed and breakfasts in Seattle allow visitors to explore the city with free bike rentals or take advantage of local hiking trails and outdoor sports. Many bed and breakfasts also provide special packages and discounts to guests, such as discounts for extended stays, discounted rates for local attractions, and discounts for nearby restaurants.

Seattle boasts a wide range of bed and breakfasts to suit your needs. A bed and breakfast stay in Seattle may be a genuinely unforgettable experience due to its distinct environment, outstanding facilities, and customised service.

Bed & Breakfasts are an excellent choice for tourists seeking a more intimate and personal experience. B&Bs in Seattle range from ancient properties to contemporary lofts. Depending on the location, several B&Bs provide free parking and breakfast. Hotel Sorrento, Inn at the Market, and The Ballard Inn are among the most popular B&Bs in Seattle.

# Motels

For tourists searching for a pleasant, reasonable, and convenient accommodation option, Seattle is an excellent choice. Seattle offers a diverse choice of motels, from budget-friendly corporations to luxurious boutique hotels.

There are numerous major chain motels in Seattle that provide reasonable prices for individuals on a tight budget. These include Days Inn and Super 8, which provide comfortable, clean rooms for $60-$90 per night on average. Free Wi-Fi, free continental breakfast, free parking, and pet-friendly accommodations are common amenities.

Seattle has a number of boutique motels for visitors looking for a more premium stay. The Inn at the Market and the Alexis Hotel are two examples. Both provide upmarket rooms with high-end facilities like flat-screen TVs, rainfall showers, and free Wi-Fi. The nightly rates vary from $100 to $300.

If you want to stay somewhere out of the ordinary, Seattle provides a few options. For example, the Green Tortoise Hostel has individual rooms, communal dormitories, and camping areas. The nightly rates vary from $29 to $99 USD. Caboose accommodations with bunk beds, private toilets, and a view of the railway tracks are available at the Northwest Railway Museum in Snoqualmie. The nightly rates vary from $99 to $139.

There are a handful of themed hotels in Seattle for people looking for a genuinely unique experience. The Fantasy Inn and the Space Needle Hotel, for example, both provide rooms with amusing themes. Rates per night vary from $99 to $250, depending on the accommodation.

Whatever type of lodging you prefer, Seattle has something to suit your budget and lifestyle. There is a motel in Seattle to fit any traveller's requirements, from budget-friendly franchises to luxury boutique motels.

## Extended Stay Hotels

Seattle has a number of extended stay hotels for travellers searching for a longer stay. Extended stay hotels have fully equipped kitchens, sitting spaces, and separate bedrooms. Popular extended stay hotels in Seattle include the Homewood Suites by Hilton Seattle, Staypineapple at Hotel Max, and the Residence Inn by Marriott Seattle.

Apartment hotels in Seattle provide long-term accommodations for guests, generally for a minimum of one week. These apartments are completely furnished and provide amenities such as kitchens, separate bedrooms and living areas, and laundry facilities. Prices vary from $100 to $200 each night, depending on the size and location of the unit. Daily cleaning is provided, as is free Wi-Fi. There are other hotels that encourage extended stay in the country.

# Resorts

Resorts are an excellent place to relax and take in the sights of Seattle. Seattle offers a range of resorts to select from, whether you're searching for a romantic break, a family holiday, or a group event. There are resorts to suit every need and budget, from luxury resorts with spa facilities to budget-friendly rooms with minimal amenities.

The cost of resorts in Seattle varies substantially based on the season, location, and facilities provided. A normal accommodation in a resort will typically cost between $200 and $400 per night. A premium resort in a beautiful location might cost up to $1000 per night, but you normally receive extras like spa treatments, room service, and other perks.

Most Seattle resorts include a wide range of services and facilities, including swimming pools, fitness centres, restaurants, shops, and more. Some of the more well-known resorts also have on-site activities such as golf courses, tennis courts, and other recreational areas. Many resorts also offer discounted packages that include transportation, meals, and other activities.

Whether you want a deluxe hideaway or an economical break, Seattle offers a resort to suit your requirements. You're sure to discover the right resort for your next Seattle trip with a broad selection of pricing and amenities to pick from.

# Luxury Suites

Some of the most magnificent suites in the United States may be found in Seattle. From the world-class facilities to the breathtaking city views, these suites provide an unrivalled experience for visitors seeking the best in luxury and comfort.

<u>The Fairmont Olympic Hotel</u> ranks first in Seattle for luxury suites. The suites of the Fairmont Olympic range from the Deluxe Suite to the Presidential Suite. The suites all include a sumptuous king-size bed, a sitting area with a gas fireplace, and a luxurious marble bathroom. You may enjoy the ultimate luxury experience with a full-service spa, great restaurants, and a rooftop pool and hot tub.Starting at **$549** per night, the Fairmont Olympic Hotel features exquisite rooms, 24-hour room service, a range of great dining options, and a full-service spa.

<u>The Four Seasons Hotel Seattle:</u> is another excellent choice for luxury suites in Seattle. This hotel has a range of suites available, from the Deluxe Suite to the Presidential Suite. Each suite has a living room with a gas fireplace, a separate bedroom, and a luxury bathroom. You may enjoy a genuinely opulent stay with an on-site spa, great restaurants, and a fitness facility. Rooms start at $539 per night and include breathtaking city views, a world-class spa, and an on-site restaurant.

**The Royal Sonesta Hotel:** is another excellent choice for luxury suites in Seattle. This hotel has a range of suites available, from the Deluxe Suite to the Presidential Suite. Each suite has a king-size bed, a living room with a gas fireplace, and a luxury bathroom. You may enjoy a genuinely opulent stay with an on-site spa, great restaurants, and a fitness facility.

**The W Seattle:** is a contemporary and trendy hotel with some of Seattle's most luxury rooms. The suites of the W Seattle range from the Deluxe Suite to the Presidential Suite. The suites are all equipped with a living area with a gas fireplace, a separate bedroom, and a beautiful bathroom. You may enjoy the ultimate luxury experience with an on-site spa, great restaurants, and a rooftop pool and hot tub. Starting at **$359** a night, this hotel features luxury rooms, an outdoor pool, and proximity to the city's bustling nightlife.

**The Ritz-Carlton Seattle:** is an excellent alternative for anyone seeking an ultra-luxurious stay. This hotel has a range of suites available, from the Deluxe Suite to the Presidential Suite. Each suite has a living room with a gas fireplace, a separate bedroom, and a luxury bathroom. You may enjoy the ultimate luxury experience with an on-site spa, great restaurants, and a fitness facility.

**Kimpton Alexis Hotel:** Starting at **$339** a night, this modern, luxurious hotel features a rooftop bar and convenient access to Seattle's lively downtown.

**Grand Hyatt Seattle:** The Grand Hyatt Seattle is a magnificent hotel in the city's centre. The renowned Space Needle and other prominent sites such as Pike Place Market, the Seattle Aquarium, and the Seattle Art Museum are all within walking distance of the hotel. Prices start at $329 per night and the hotel's rooms and suites are large and elegantly decorated, with contemporary conveniences. Guests may unwind with a number of leisure options, including a 24-hour fitness facility and a rooftop pool. Guests may also choose from a choice of delectable dining alternatives, such as the award-winning Grand Hyatt Seattle restaurant, which serves a selection of local seafood and Pacific Northwest favourites. The concierge service at the hotel is accessible 24 hours a day to assist guests with any needs they may have.

**Mayflower Park Hotel:** The Mayflower Park Hotel is a premium downtown Seattle hotel. The Seattle Aquarium, Pike Place Market, and the renowned Space Needle are all within walking distance of the hotel. Starting at $299 per night, the hotel offers big and pleasant rooms and suites with contemporary conveniences. Guests may take use of a variety of recreational amenities, including a fitness centre and an indoor pool. Guests may also dine at the award-winning Mayflower Park Restaurant, which serves a range of local seafood and Pacific Northwest delicacies. The concierge service at the hotel is accessible 24 hours a day to assist guests with any needs they may have.

**Hotel 1000:** Located in the centre of downtown Seattle, Hotel 1000 is a magnificent hotel. The renowned Space Needle and other prominent sites such as Pike Place Market, the Seattle Aquarium, and the Seattle Art Museum are all within walking distance of the hotel. The hotel offers contemporary, spacious rooms and suites with modern conveniences. Guests may unwind with a range of leisure activities, including the 24-hour fitness facility and rooftop pool. Guests may also take advantage of a choice of delectable eating options, including the award-winning Hotel 1000 restaurant, which serves a variety of local seafood and Pacific Northwest favourites. The concierge service at the hotel is accessible 24 hours a day to assist guests with any needs they may have.Rooms start at $449 per night

**Sheraton Grand Seattle:** Located in the centre of downtown Seattle, the Sheraton Grand Seattle is a magnificent hotel. The Seattle Aquarium, Pike Place Market, and the renowned Space Needle are all within walking distance of the hotel. The hotel offers big and pleasant rooms and suites with contemporary conveniences. Guests may take use of a variety of recreational amenities, including a fitness centre and an indoor pool. Guests may also dine at the award-winning Sheraton Grand Seattle restaurant, which serves a selection of local seafood and Pacific Northwest delicacies. The concierge service at the hotel is accessible 24 hours a day to assist guests with any needs they may have.

**Seattle Marriott Waterfront Luxury Hotel:** Located on the waterfront in downtown Seattle, the Seattle Marriott Waterfront is a magnificent hotel. The Seattle Aquarium, Pike Place Market, and the renowned Space Needle are all within walking distance of the hotel. The hotel offers big and pleasant rooms and suites with contemporary conveniences. Guests may take use of a variety of recreational amenities, including a fitness centre and an indoor pool. Guests may also dine at the award-winning Seattle Marriott Waterfront restaurant, which serves a selection of local seafood and Pacific Northwest delicacies. The concierge service at the hotel is accessible 24 hours a day to assist guests with any needs they may have.Rooms start at $449 per night.

# CHAPTER 5: EXPLORING SEATTLE

Begin your journey by strolling around Pike Place Market, the United States' longest continuously functioning farmers' market. You may try local cuisine and buy fresh fruit and one-of-a-kind presents here. After that, go down the shoreline and take in the breathtaking vistas of Puget Sound and the Olympic Mountains.There's lots to see and do whether you're here for a weekend or a longer stay. Seattle has something for everyone, from outdoor activities to various neighbourhoods to a lively culture.

Whatever you choose to do in Seattle, you will have a memorable time. So, what are you holding out for? Explore Seattle and experience all it has to offer.

## Must-See Attractions

Seattle, Washington, is one of the most beautiful cities in the United States, with a plethora of things to visit. Whether you're searching for culture, nature, or simply a good time, Seattle offers something for everyone.

Here are some of Seattle's must-see attractions and their prices:

**1. _Space Needle:_** A 605-foot-tall building situated in the centre of Seattle, the Space Needle is one of the city's most famous monuments. The observation platform at the summit offers breathtaking views of the city and the surrounding mountains. Admission to the Space Needle is $19.99 for adults, $17.99 for seniors, $14.99 for juniors, and free for children 5 and under.

**2. _Pike Place Market:_** Founded in 1907, Pike Place Market is Seattle's oldest public market. Fresh fruit, artists selling their handcrafted crafts, and some of the greatest seafood in the city can all be found here. The market is completely free to enter.

**3. _Seattle Aquarium:_** Located on Pier 59, the Seattle Aquarium is home to a vast variety of aquatic life, including sharks, whales, seals, and more. The aquarium also provides educational events and interactive displays. Admission to the Seattle Aquarium is $34.95 for adults, $29.95 for seniors, $24.95 for children, and free for children under the age of four.

**4. The Seattle Great Wheel:** The Seattle Great Wheel is a massive Ferris wheel situated on Pier 57. The observation wheel provides breathtaking views of the city, Elliott Bay, and the Olympic Mountains. Admission to the Seattle Great Wheel is $13 for adults, $11 for seniors, and $9 for children.

**5. Seattle Art Museum:** The Seattle Art Museum has an extraordinary collection of artwork from throughout the globe. The museum also conducts special events and exhibits throughout the year. Admission to the museum is $25 for adults, $22 for seniors, $19 for students and adolescents, and free for children 12 and under.

**6. Chihuly Garden and Glass:** Located in the Seattle Center, the Chihuly Garden and Glass is a magnificent collection of glass sculptures made by famous artist Dale Chihuly. The garden has an outdoor garden, an interior gallery, and a theatre. The Chihuly Garden and Glass cost $29 for adults, $26 for seniors, $23 for students and adolescents, and free for children 5 and under.

**7. Museum of Pop Culture (MoPOP):** The Museum of Pop Culture is a one-of-a-kind museum situated in the Seattle Center. Explore the history of music, movies, video games, and more. Admission to MoPOP is $28 for adults, $25 for seniors, $22 for students and adolescents, and free for children 5 and under.

These are just a handful of the numerous attractions in Seattle. Whether you're searching for culture, nature, or simply a good time, Seattle offers something for everyone.

# Popular Neighbourhoods

## Pioneer Square

Pioneer Square is a historic area in the centre of Seattle, Washington. It is one of the city's oldest neighbourhoods, going back to the mid-1800s when Seattle was founded. It was the city's first commercial sector, and it remains an essential part of its history.

### Places To Visit

Pioneer Square is now a dynamic, busy district packed with interesting stores, restaurants, and art galleries. It is home to some of Seattle's most recognizable structures, including the

Pioneer Building, Smith Tower, and the Klondike Gold Rush National Historical Park. There are many public art pieces in Seattle, including the Seattle Firefighters Memorial and the Seattle Totem Pole. The Klondike Gold Rush National Historical Park, which houses numerous relics from the late 1800s gold rush, is also located in the area.

## Activities

Pioneer Square is an excellent location for exploring and experiencing Seattle's rich history. Throughout the year, there are a variety of activities and events to enjoy, such as the monthly First Thursday Art Walk, Saturday Farmers Market, and Sunday Art Walk. The area also hosts a number of festivals and events, such as the Bite of Seattle, the Fremont Oktoberfest, and the Seattle International Film Festival.

Occidental Park, located in the area, offers a range of recreational activities, including walking and bike routes, a skate park, and a playground. The park also hosts a variety of cultural events, including the annual Solstice Parade and the Folklife Festival.

Pioneer Square is one of Seattle's most distinct and dynamic districts. With its rich history, distinctive shops and restaurants, and a variety of activities and events, it's simple to understand why this area is a terrific destination to come and explore.

## Fremont

The Fremont area of Seattle, Washington is noted for its varied culture, energetic environment, and abundance of activities. Fremont, located just north of the Lake Washington Ship Canal, is a favourite location for tourists searching for a unique experience in the Emerald City.

### Nightlife and shopping

Fremont is recognized for its vibrant street life, vivid murals, and one-of-a-kind art galleries. The Fremont Sunday Market is a famous weekly event that features local merchants offering fresh vegetables, homemade products, and other items. The Fremont area also holds a number of events throughout the year, including the Fremont Solstice Parade, the Fremont Oktoberfest, and the Fremont Fair.

## Places & Activities

Fremont is home to a number of attractions, including the Fremont Troll, a massive sculpture of a troll that dwells under the Aurora Bridge. Another famous site is the Fremont Rocket, a Cold War-era rocket-shaped monument that towers over the area. The Fremont Brewing Company, a prominent craft brewery, and the Fremont Abbey Arts Center, a nonprofit venue for music, dance, theatre, and art, are both located in the area.

The Burke-Gilman Trail passes through Fremont and is a fantastic place to enjoy the outdoors. There are also various parks in the region, including Gas Works Park, a favourite site for picnics and BBQs, and Fremont Peak Park, which gives amazing views of Seattle and the Sound.

Fremont is a fantastic area for exploring Seattle's distinct culture and enjoying the various activities on offer. Whether you're searching for an outdoor adventure or a unique cultural experience, Fremont offers something for everyone.

# The Waterfront

The waterfront neighbourhood in Seattle is a vibrant and lively area bustling with activity. Located along the Puget Sound, this area is home to some of the city's most popular attractions, including the Seattle Aquarium, the Seattle Great Wheel, and the iconic Pike Place Market.

The waterfront also offers plenty of outdoor activities and entertainment, such as kayaking, biking, and fishing.

The views from the waterfront are breathtaking. From the shore, visitors can take in the beauty of the Seattle skyline and the Olympic Mountains. The waterfront is also home to some of the city's most popular restaurants, cafes, and bars. Visitors can enjoy the freshest seafood and other local favourites, as well as craft cocktails and beers from the area's many breweries.

In the summer months, the waterfront comes alive with festivals, concerts, and other events. The Seattle Waterfront Music Festival is a popular event that takes place every summer, featuring some of the best local and international acts. Visitors can also take part in the Waterfront 5K, an annual running event that is held in May.

No matter what time of year, there is something to do in the waterfront neighbourhood. Whether you're looking for a relaxing stroll along the pier or a night out on the town, the waterfront has something for everyone.

## Downtown Seattle

Downtown Seattle is the city's core and most popular district, offering breathtaking views of Puget Sound and the Seattle skyline. Take a walk around Pike Place Market, visit Olympic Sculpture Park, and ride the Great Wheel for panoramic views of the city. From the historic Public Market to the landmark Space Needle, there's plenty of shopping, dining, and nightlife choices. It's a thriving and lively district at the city's core. It is well-known for its vibrant ambiance, stylish restaurants and bars, and a diverse range of attractions and activities.

Downtown Seattle boasts a wide range of shopping opportunities, from upscale merchants to neighbourhood boutiques. It is home to the historic Seattle Public Library and the iconic Pike Place Market, where you can discover a variety of fresh vegetables and unusual goods. The neighbourhood is also recognized for its various theatres, museums, and galleries, which provide something for everyone.

The Seattle Center is a fantastic location for outdoor activities, festivals, and cultural attractions. The Space Needle, the Seattle Children's Museum, the Pacific Science Center, the Chihuly Garden and Glass, and the Seattle Opera are all located there..

## Capitol Hill

Capitol Hill is a dynamic, active, and varied area in the centre of Seattle with a rich history, culture, and entertainment opportunities. Capitol Hill offers something for everyone, from its early days as a residential district for the city's aristocracy to its present standing as one of the city's trendiest locations to live.

### Nightlife & Shopping

The area is recognized for its active nightlife, which includes numerous prominent pubs and clubs along Broadway, Pike, and Pine, as well as its diverse restaurants, coffee shops, and boutiques. There are also art galleries, museums, theatres, and music venues dotted around the area, offering a range of entertainment alternatives.Capitol Hill is a lively area with an active nightlife. Some of Seattle's best music venues, bars, and restaurants can be found here. There are a range of cuisines available here, ranging from conventional American meals to delectable Asian fusion. People travel long distances to see unique stores and boutiques.

## Places to visit

The Seattle Central Library, situated on Capitol Hill, is a work of art and a popular attraction for both residents and tourists. The library has a wide collection of books and other media, as well as a range of activities such as live music and talks.

Volunteer Park and Cal Anderson Park, which hold a range of activities like outdoor concerts, movies, festivals, and other events, are also located in the area. Parks are also popular areas for individuals to unwind, take a stroll, or just enjoy the city views.

## Activities

Capitol Hill also has a thriving LGBTQ+ culture, with several clubs, restaurants, and cafés catering to the group. Every year, thousands of people from all over the globe attend Seattle

Pride, a prominent annual celebration of the LGBTQ+ community.

Capitol Hill is a fantastic area to live, with lots of events and entertainment to keep you entertained all year. Capitol Hill is a terrific area to live, with its active nightlife and cultural activities, parks and green spaces, and inclusive LGBTQ+ community.

## Ballard

The Ballard neighbourhood of Seattle is one of the most popular neighbourhoods in the city. This vibrant community is full of interesting culture, great food, and plenty of activities.

### Nightlife & Shopping

Ballard is best known for its lively nightlife, which includes plenty of bars and restaurants. The area is home to some of Seattle's most popular dive bars, including the iconic White Horse Tavern, The Little Red Hen, and The Sunset. There are also a number of upscale restaurants, such as the hip steakhouse Shaker & Spear, the Mediterranean-inspired Ocho, and the seafood specialists The Walrus and the Carpenter. Ballard also boasts a thriving craft beer and wine scene.

The Ballard neighbourhood is also home to a number of unique boutiques, galleries, and antique stores. Shop for home goods at the iconic Scandinavian Specialties, find unique gifts at the Ballard Sunday Market, and browse vintage clothing at Seattle's first vintage store, Metrix.

## Places to visit

For those seeking outdoor activities, Ballard is a great place to explore. The neighbourhood is home to several parks, including Ballard Commons Park and Golden Gardens Park. Ballard Commons Park is a popular spot for picnics, walking, and a variety of outdoor activities. Golden Gardens Park is a secluded beach with stunning views of the Puget Sound and the Olympic Mountains.

## Activities

Ballard is also home to a number of festivals and events throughout the year. Ballard SeafoodFest is a two-day event that celebrates the neighbourhood's fishing industry and the annual Ballard Jazz Festival is a popular event that brings together local and international jazz musicians.

No matter what you're looking for, Ballard has something for everyone. Whether you're looking for a night out on the town, a unique shopping experience, or a relaxing day outdoors, Ballard has it all.

## University District

The University District area of Seattle, Washington is one of the city's most active and varied neighbourhoods. The University District, just north of Downtown Seattle, is home to the University of Washington, Seattle's biggest university and one of the top educational institutions in the nation. The area is also home to a diverse range of restaurants, stores, and nightlife, making it a popular destination for both residents and tourists.

### Activities

Throughout the year, the University District is a hive of activity. During the summer, it's one of the best places in the city to experience Seattle's famous music and arts scene. There's always something going on in the University District, from street performers to live concerts to local art displays. During the school year, the area is teeming with college students, making it a terrific spot to grab a snack or spend the night.

## Nightlife & Shopping

If you like shopping, the University District has a variety of options, ranging from antique apparel stores to trendy boutiques. There are also many restaurants to select from, including a range of ethnic cuisines. Check out the University District Farmers Market, which is held every Sunday from May through October.

When it comes to nightlife, the University District has something to offer everyone. There are lots of locations to get a drink and dance the night away, ranging from live music venues to pubs. There are also a variety of comedy clubs, karaoke bars, and other entertainment locations to pick from.

## Places To Visit

The University District also has a multitude of parks and open areas, making it a perfect spot to unwind and enjoy the outdoors. The University of Washington campus is surrounded by beautiful gardens, walking pathways, and a variety of open green areas. Nearby parks include the Burke-Gilman Trail, Gas Works Park, and Volunteer Park.

Whether you're searching for a night out, some shopping, or a quiet spot to unwind, the University District is one of Seattle's most fascinating and active areas. It's a terrific area to visit or live because of its combination of college students, culture, and entertainment.

# Off The Beaten Path (hidden gems).

Seattle is a city full of hidden gems, offering visitors a wealth of activities and attractions to explore that are often overlooked by the average traveller. From the city's bustling Pike Place Market and iconic Space Needle to its many hidden attractions, Seattle is a great place to discover something new. From hidden gardens to secret bars and speakeasies, there's plenty to uncover in the Emerald City.

**Olympic Sculpture Park:** is one of the best hidden gems in Seattle. This 9-acre park was created by the Seattle Art Museum in 2007 and features stunning sculptures, fountains, and gardens set against the backdrop of Puget Sound and the Olympic Mountains. The park is free to visit and open year-round, making it a great destination for a leisurely stroll.

**The Fremont Troll:** is another one of Seattle's hidden gems. This 18-foot concrete troll sculpture was created in 1990 and can be found under the Aurora Bridge in the Fremont neighbourhood. The troll is an iconic Seattle landmark and is often the site of public art shows and festivals.

**The Ballard Locks:** If you're looking for a unique experience, the Ballard Locks are a must-visit. The Ballard Locks are a set of locks on the Ship Canal connecting Puget Sound to Lake Union. The locks are a popular spot for watching boats pass through and are also home to the famous fish ladder, which allows salmon to safely migrate between the two bodies of water.

**The Seattle Underground:** is also a unique hidden gem in the city. The underground was created in 1889 after a fire destroyed most of the downtown area. Visitors can take a tour of the underground and explore the hidden passageways, tunnels, and storefronts from the 19th century.

**The Knee High Stocking Company:** is a great place to check out for a unique nightlife experience. The speakeasy is located in the Chinatown-International District and is hidden behind a secret door. Inside, you'll find a cosy lounge with a full bar and live music. The Knee

High Stocking Company is a great spot for an evening of drinks and dancing.

These are just a few of the hidden gems located in Seattle. Whether you're looking for outdoor activities or a unique nightlife experience, Seattle has something for everyone. So get out there and explore the city's many hidden gems.

# Culinary (local) Experiences

Seattle is a dynamic city in the United States' Pacific Northwest. Seattle, often known as the Emerald City, is famed for its magnificent natural beauty, lively culture, and many attractions. Seattle offers something for everyone, from the famous Space Needle to the busy Pike Place Market.

**Seattle Neighbourhoods:** There are several possibilities for people interested in experiencing Seattle's local culture. Seattle has numerous thriving neighbourhoods, each with its own distinct character.

The University District has a varied mix of stores and eateries, while Capitol Hill is an excellent location for exploring the city's art scene. Both Ballard and Fremont are recognized for their independent stores and eateries, while Pioneer Square and Chinatown provide a glimpse into the city's past.

**Outdoor Activities:** Outdoor lovers will enjoy the various outdoor activities available in Seattle. Mount Rainier and Olympic National Park are two of the country's most beautiful national parks, both located near Seattle. Hiking, biking, and kayaking are among popular activities in Seattle. During the summer, residents can swim at Alki Beach or take a boat to the San Juan Islands.

**Music & Art:** Seattle boasts a thriving music and art scene as well. Many well-known music venues, such as the Showbox and the Crocodile, can be found in the city. The Seattle Art Museum, the Frye Art Museum, and the Henry Art Gallery are all excellent venues to learn about the art of the area.

**Top Restaurants:** Seattle has some of the top restaurants in the nation for people searching for unique culinary experiences. Seattle's food ranges from high-end establishments like Canlis to more informal cafes like Paseo. The city is also recognized for its coffee culture, including notable cafés such as Starbucks, Victrola, and Top Pot.

Seattle is a city full of vitality and possibilities for both residents and tourists. Seattle is a terrific city to visit and experience, with its gorgeous environment, active culture, and many attractions.

## Museums

Seattle is a dynamic city rich in culture, from the famous Space Needle to the many museums that attract people from all over the globe. From the world-renowned Seattle Art Museum to the Museum of History and Industry, Seattle's museums provide something for everyone. Whether you want to study about the city's rich history, learn about its varied culture, or just admire some gorgeous artwork, Seattle's museums offer it all.

**The Museum of History and Industry (MOHAI):** is committed to preserving and promoting Seattle's and its people's history. MOHAI's permanent displays feature a chronicle of the city's history, as well as a look at the city's maritime, music, and technology sectors. MOHAI also hosts temporary exhibits that address issues ranging from the city's urban development to its famed sports teams.

**The Burke Museum of Natural History and Culture:** is the state of Washington's oldest museum. It displays a diverse range of artefacts, including dinosaur fossils and Native American artefacts. The museum also provides a range of educational activities such as guided tours, seminars, and courses.

**Living Computer Museum:** is another wonderful Museum in Seattle. It contains a large collection of computers, ranging from early versions such as the IBM PC to the most recent Apple devices. Visitors may learn about the history of computing technology, from its inception to the present day, and even get hands-on experience with the computers on show.

Below we explain in detail some of the most visited and finest museums.

## Seattle Art Museum

The Seattle Art Museum (SAM) is one of the greatest and finest museums in the Pacific Northwest, with something for everyone. The museum, located in downtown Seattle, has nearly 25,000 pieces of art from throughout the globe. There is a vast spectrum of art to discover, from antique sculptures to modern and contemporary items.

## Galleries

The museum has a number of galleries, including the Asian Art Museum, the European Painting Gallery, and the American Art Museum, to mention a few. Each gallery provides a comprehensive look into the region's culture and history. Additionally, the museum hosts several special exhibitions throughout the year, including the Seattle Biennial and the Seattle Art Fair.

## Events

The museum also offers a range of events, such as talks, courses, and workshops. These range from youth art classes to adult lectures on various art-related topics. The museum also sponsors a number of events and festivals, such as the Seattle International Film Festival, the Seattle Design Festival, and the Seattle Asian Art Museum Festival.

## Collections

The museum also features a range of interactive displays, such as "Art in Motion," which enables visitors to examine the artwork in the galleries in a novel manner. The museum also contains a variety of interactive exhibits, such as the "Sculpture Garden" and the "Ceramics Lab," that enable visitors to engage with the artwork.

The Seattle Art Museum is a fantastic destination to explore and learn about art from across the globe. There is something for everyone among its galleries, special exhibitions, and interactive displays.

## Museum of Pop Culture

The Museum of Pop Culture, or MoPOP, is an interactive museum in Seattle, Washington committed to investigating the creativity and invention of popular culture. The museum was created in 2000 by Microsoft co-founder Paul Allen and contains a diverse collection of exhibits focusing on popular music, science fiction and fantasy, horror, and video games. MoPOP also provides a range of special events, such as concerts, movie screenings, talks, and workshops.

### Collection

The Science Fiction & Fantasy Hall of Fame, the Indie Game Revolution, and the Infinite Worlds of Science Fiction are among the numerous permanent exhibitions in the museum that study popular culture. Other permanent displays look at horror and fantasy literature, cinema, and television, as well as the history of video gaming. The museum also offers rotating exhibits that concentrate on certain subjects, such as the current exhibition on the history and impact of hip-hop.

### Attraction & Events

MoPOP also includes a number of additional attractions in addition to its displays. Visitors may tour the museum's sound lab and recording studio, attend special events and performances, and participate in a range of courses and seminars. The museum also has its own theatre, which organises screenings of classic films as well as live performances by local artists.

## The museum of flight

The Museum of Flight, located in Seattle, Washington, is one of the world's biggest and most comprehensive aviation and space museums. The museum, which has been open since 1965, is situated on the old Boeing plant and airport grounds. It is a non-profit organisation committed to preserving and presenting aviation and space exploration heritage.

## Collection

The Museum of Flight provides a range of exhibits, exhibitions, and interactive activities for visitors. It includes a diverse collection of aircraft on exhibit, ranging from the first days of flying to current jets employed by the military and commercial airlines. The museum also has a collection of artefacts and papers that chronicle the narrative of aviation's growth.

The Museum of flying also has an aviation library with over 100,000 books and a research centre dedicated to the history of flying. The library has original source materials including pictures, drawings, and manuscripts, as well as secondary sources like books, periodicals, and journals.

## Events & Activities

In addition, the museum provides a range of educational events for both children and adults. In interactive exhibits, visitors can participate in hands-on activities, watch lectures, and learn about the history of aviation. Throughout the year, the museum also hosts special events and programs such as air shows, film festivals, and exhibitions.

The Museum of Flight is open every day of the year and entry is free. It also features a gift store, café, and restaurant, as well as group trips. The museum is a popular location for student field excursions and an excellent site to learn about aviation and space exploration history.

# Theater

Seattle has a wide range of theatres, from tiny independent venues to large-scale performing arts facilities. Aside from its many theatres, Seattle is also home to a number of film festivals and special events.

**The Seattle Repertory Theatre**: one of the major regional theatres in the United States, is one of the city's most notable theatres. Throughout the year, the theatre stages a variety of plays, musicals, and other performances. The Seattle Repertory Theatre, situated in the Seattle Center, is one of the most prominent theatre and performing arts venues in the region.

**The 5th Avenue Theatre:** is another well-known Seattle theatre. This ancient theatre, which initially opened in 1926, is now one of the most popular venues in the city. Throughout the year, the theatre hosts a variety of musicals, plays, and special events. The Seattle International Dance Festival, one of the biggest dance festivals in the country, is also held in the theatre.

**The Paramount Theatre:** is another prominent venue in Seattle. This theatre was erected in 1928 and is one of the city's most iconic structures. Throughout the year, the theatre hosts a variety of plays and musicals, and it also serves as the home of the Seattle Symphony Orchestra.

**The Neptune Theatre:** is another prominent venue in Seattle. This theatre in the University District is well-known for its collection of independent films, concerts, and other live entertainment. The theatre also hosts a number of special events throughout the year, including the Seattle International Film Festival.

**Moore Theatre:** is another well-known Seattle theatre. This theatre was founded in 1907 and is one of the city's oldest. The theatre hosts a variety of concerts, plays, and other events throughout the year.

**The Seattle Center:** has a number of theatres and performing arts venues. The Seattle Center is home to the Seattle Opera, Pacific Northwest Ballet, and other performing arts groups. The Seattle Center also organises a number of festivals and events throughout the year, such as the Bite of Seattle and the Folklife Festival.

Seattle is also home to a number of independent theatres and performing venues. These venues vary in size and scope, but they all host a variety of performances and events throughout the year. These venues, which are often situated in neighbourhoods, are an excellent opportunity to immerse yourself in Seattle's cultural and art scene.

# Cultural Festivals & Events

Seattle is a bustling city full of culture and activity, with several festivals and events held throughout the year. There is something for everyone, from music festivals to art fairs.

During the summer, Seattle hosts a number of cultural festivals that highlight the city's diverse population. The Seattle International Film Festival is the Northwest's biggest and most distinguished film festival, showcasing films from all over the globe. There's also Bumbershoot, a music and arts festival held in Seattle every year since 1971. This music and arts event showcases hundreds of international bands, DJs, and performers, as well as a variety of art and food exhibitors.

Another prominent summer event in Seattle is the Fremont Fair and Solstice Parade. This fair features local artists, entertainers, and sellers, as well as a parade with bright costumes and colourful floats to commemorate the longest day of the year. In July, the Capitol Hill Block Party features some of the best indie and electronic music around. Seattle celebrates its rich cultural history in August with the Nihonmachi Street Fair, a two-day festival including traditional Japanese dishes and entertainment, and Seattle Pride, an annual LGBTQ celebration.

The Bite of Seattle, which takes place in the autumn and comprises over 60 restaurants and food exhibitors, is a popular event for foodies. The Seattle Earshot Jazz Festival features concerts by local and international musicians, while the Folklife Festival features traditional music, dance, and culture from throughout the globe. Every year, the Seattle Asian Art

Museum presents the Sakura-Con Anime and Manga Convention.

Winter in Seattle is all about holiday celebrations. The Fremont Winter Solstice Parade is a colourful parade of people and puppets celebrating the winter solstice, while the Seattle Center Snow Day provides guests with a day of snow activities and entertainment. Woodland Park Zoo's Wildlights is a Christmas light show that draws people from all across the area.

Seattle is a culturally diverse city with something for everyone all year. There's always something to do in Seattle, whether you're searching for music festivals, art fairs, or holiday festivities.

# CHAPTER 6: DINING IN SEATTLE

Dining in Seattle is an unforgettable experience. Seattle offers something for everyone, from the finest seafood to the most delectable Asian cuisine. The city's food reflects its melting pot of cultures and cuisines. When it comes to seafood, Seattle is unrivalled. Seattle has some of the finest seafood in the country, from the legendary salmon to crab, oysters, mussels, and more. Pike Place Market is a great place to buy the freshest seafood right from the fisherman.

If you want something more exotic, go to the International District. A variety of Asian restaurants provide foods from Korea, Japan, China, Thailand, and other countries. The International District provides something for everyone, from traditional foods to fusion cuisine.

For something a little more informal, there are plenty of gastropubs and pubs in Seattle dishing up comfort cuisine with a twist. These establishments often feature excellent beer and wine options, as well as live music.

Whatever type of cuisine you're looking for, Seattle is sure to have something to satisfy your taste buds. Seattle offers it all, whether you're looking for a romantic supper, a relaxed lunch, or a fast nibble.

# Restaurants In Seattle.

**1. <u>Fine Dining:</u>** These establishments provide the greatest level of cuisine, service, and environment. They often serve numerous courses and are frequently regarded as the most costly restaurants in a certain region. Canlis and The Herbfarm are two examples in Seattle.There are a few restaurants that stand out as the most popular in Seattle. These restaurants provide a broad range of services, from conventional American food to new twists on classic meals.

**The Pink Door -** is the first that springs to mind. This small Italian restaurant in Pike Place Market serves delectable Italian comfort cuisine including homemade pastas, antipasti, and wood-fired pizzas. Craft cocktails, local beers, and wines are also available. The Pink Door's ambience is quiet and welcoming, with a nice outside terrace and a big collection of paintings and photography on the walls.

**The Walrus and the Carpenter -** is another renowned Seattle eatery. This seafood-focused restaurant in Ballard serves fresh, local fish. They provide a wide range of foods, from exquisite oysters to inventive seafood dishes. The ambiance is welcoming and pleasant, with an emphasis on sustainability.

**The 5 Point Cafe -** is the place to go for a traditional American diner experience. This Seattle institution has been serving basic dinner meals like burgers and fries for over a century. The ambience is relaxed and easygoing, with an emphasis on comfort and nostalgia.

**The Dahlia Lounge -** offers a flavour of contemporary Seattle. This Pike Place Market restaurant serves sophisticated Northwest cuisine with an emphasis on local, sustainable ingredients. They provide a range of foods, including wood-fired pizzas, salads, and sandwiches. With an open kitchen and a bar area, the environment is contemporary and stylish.

**Canlis** - Located in the centre of Seattle, Canlis is widely regarded as the city's greatest restaurant. It is a family-run business that has been servicing Seattle for over 70 years. Canlis provides upmarket dining with contemporary American cuisine. Each meal is meticulously prepared with fresh, local ingredients. The wine list at the restaurant is equally remarkable, featuring options from all around the globe. Canlis is also noted for providing excellent service and paying close attention to detail.

**The Whale Wins** - A quiet restaurant in Seattle's Fremont area, The Whale Wins is great for a dating night. Seasonal New American food like roasted pork shoulder, pan-roasted halibut, and roasted carrots with harissa yoghourt are on the menu. The Whale Wins also features a good assortment of craft beers and wines.

**Lecosho** - Located in downtown Seattle, Lecosho is a contemporary American restaurant. The menu includes items such as smoked pig loin, grilled octopus, and risotto with roasted mushrooms. In addition, the restaurant offers an amazing assortment of artisan beers and wines.

**2. Casual Dining:** These restaurants provide a less formal setting than fine dining while yet providing outstanding cuisine and service. Red Robin and The Cheesecake Factory are two Seattle examples.

**3. Quick Service:** These eateries provide quick, convenient, and typically economical meals. Subway and Taco Bell are two examples from Seattle.

**4. Fast Casual:** These restaurants give greater variety and personalization than quick service restaurants while still offering speedy service. Chipotle and Panera Bread are two examples from Seattle.

**5. Cafes:** These establishments provide coffee, tea, and other drinks as well as light appetisers. Starbucks and Top Pot Doughnuts are two Seattle examples.

**6. Takeout:** These restaurants provide cuisine that is designed to be carried away and consumed elsewhere. In Seattle, examples include Piroshky Piroshky and India Bistro, as well as Burger King and KFC.

**7. meals Trucks:** These restaurants provide a variety of meals from a truck or cart, sometimes with a distinct theme or cuisine. In Seattle, examples are Where Ya At Matt and Street Treats.

**8. Vegetarian:** These eateries provide vegetarian and vegan dishes that are free of animal components. Wayward Vegan Cafe and Plum Bistro are two examples in Seattle.

**9. Bar & Grill:** Bar & grills are informal eateries that provide classic American pub cuisine like burgers and wings as well as beverages. T.S. McHugh's and The Pine Box are two examples of bar and grills in Seattle.

**10. Pizza Restaurant:** Pizza restaurants provide pizza as well as other Italian meals. Tutta Bella and Pagliacci Pizza are two Seattle pizza restaurants.

**11. Seafood Restaurant:** Fish and other seafood dishes are served in seafood restaurants. Ivar's and Ray's Boathouse are two Seattle seafood restaurants.

# CHAPTER 7:OUTDOOR ACTIVITIES

Seattle is an outdoor enthusiast's dream! Seattle is ideal for exploring the great outdoors, thanks to its temperate temperature and stunning vistas of the Cascade and Olympic mountain ranges. Whether you want to take a leisurely walk, a tough trek, or a thrilling adventure, Seattle offers something for everyone.

Start your outdoor excursion with a stroll or run in one of the numerous municipal parks. From the huge expanses of Discovery Park to the urban paradise of Volunteer Park, Seattle offers plenty of green space to explore. Or maybe you'd want to take a leisurely walk along the waterfront in Seattle's lovely downtown district. Here you may observe the city skyline and take in the breathtaking views of Puget Sound.

If you prefer hiking, the numerous routes in the neighbouring mountains will not disappoint. From the short treks of Rattlesnake Ledge to the hard climbs of Mt. Si and Mt. Rainier,

Seattle provides something for hikers of all abilities. Not to mention the world-famous Wonderland Trail around Mt. Rainier, a 93-mile trip through some of the most beautiful landscapes in the Pacific Northwest.

Seattle has enough to offer those searching for an adrenaline boost. There are several activities to get your heart rate up, ranging from kayaking and canoeing to rock climbing and mountain riding. If you prefer the water, you may hire a sailboat or go whitewater rafting on the neighbouring rivers.

Whatever type of outdoor adventure you seek, Seattle has something for you. In the Emerald City, you can enjoy a leisurely stroll or an adrenaline-pumping adventure.

## Parks and Garden

From lush gardens and parks to meandering paths and spectacular vistas, Seattle offers a wide range of outdoor activities and attractions. Seattle offers something for everyone, whether you want to relax and absorb nature or be active and explore.The gardens and parks of Seattle provide a diverse variety of activities and experiences. There are many paths to explore if you want to be active, from the simple and flat routes surrounding Green Lake to the more difficult trails of Snoqualmie Pass. There are lots of gardens and parks to visit if you'd prefer to simply relax and enjoy the beauty of nature. Seattle offers something for everyone, from Japanese gardens to the historic Washington Park Arboretum.

You may also take a guided tour of Seattle's various parks and gardens, or even fly above the city in a hot air balloon.

Whatever type of outdoor activity you seek, Seattle is sure to have something to offer. Seattle is the ideal destination to explore and appreciate the great outdoors, with its beautiful gardens, parks, trails, and one-of-a-kind experiences.

Some of the most gorgeous parks in the nation may be found in Seattle. There is something for everyone, from beautiful green woods to rugged shores. Here are three of Seattle's top parks to visit and the outdoor activities available in each:

**Lincoln Park:** Lincoln Park, located on the beautiful Puget Sound, is a terrific place for outdoor activities. You may hike the forest pathways and enjoy the breathtaking views of the sound. You may also take use of the many picnic sites, playgrounds, and sports fields.

Swimming, kayaking, and paddleboarding are all popular activities at the neighbouring beach.

**Discovery Park:** is one of Seattle's biggest parks, with over 500 acres of beautiful green woodlands. Explore the vast pathways and enjoy the stunning views of Puget Sound. Outdoor activities such as fishing, birding, and animal viewing are also available.

**Gas Works Park:** Gas Works Park is a 20-acre park on Lake Union's coastline. The park is well-known for its unusual industrial surroundings and spectacular lake vistas. You may go for a stroll around the lake, have a picnic, or just watch the sailboats go past. You may also engage in outdoor activities such as biking, jogging, and birding.

**Olympic Sculpture Park:** situated in Seattle's Belltown area, is a nine-acre outdoor sculpture park. The park is well-known for its spectacular vistas of Puget Sound, the Olympic Mountains, and downtown Seattle. Explore the twisting trails and see the stunning statues. Outdoor activities such as birding, bicycling, and jogging are also available. Olympic Sculpture Park is the ideal park to visit whether you want to rest or explore.

You'll have a terrific time no matter which park you visit. Seattle's parks have some of the greatest outdoor activities in the nation and are certain to provide a memorable experience. So gather your family and friends and go to one of these parks for some outdoor entertainment.

## Hiking and Biking

Seattle, Washington is a fantastic city to visit, offering a broad range of outdoor activities. Seattle offers something for everyone, from hiking and bicycling in the Cascade Mountains to kayaking and sailing on Puget Sound. There's no lack of interesting things to pick from, whether you're an experienced outdoor enthusiast or simply seeking to try something new.

**Hiking and biking:** There are various paths around Seattle that provide spectacular vistas as well as demanding terrain. The Cascade Mountains provide a range of hiking and biking paths, ranging from moderate, rolling routes to steep, challenging terrain. The adjacent Snoqualmie Pass is a popular location for bikers seeking a challenge, while Discovery Park provides a calm trail for a leisurely walk.

**Kayaking & Paddling:** Because Seattle is surrounded by water on three sides, it is an ideal location for paddle sports. The Puget Sound is home to a diverse range of species, including seals, porpoises, and eagles, and it provides breathtaking vistas of the Olympic Mountains and the Seattle cityscape. Kayaking and stand-up paddle boarding are popular pastimes, and there are several kayak rental businesses around the city.

**Sailing:** is a popular sport in Seattle, which has various sailing clubs, marinas, and charter firms. With several sheltered coves and inlets, the Puget Sound provides year-round sailing possibilities. Seattle offers something for everyone, whether you're an experienced sailor or a beginner eager to get started.

**Camping:** There are many campsites in Seattle, both in the city and in the adjacent Cascade Mountains. You'll find something to fit your requirements, whether you're searching for a basic campground or a luxurious RV park. There's something for everyone, from camping in the city's backyard to exploring the Cascades' wilderness.

**Rock climbing:** is a popular pastime in Seattle, featuring routes for climbers of all skill levels. Climbers go to the neighbouring Index Town Wall, which has climbs ranging from beginner to difficult. If you want something a little more difficult, the adjacent Leavenworth region has some of the greatest climbing in the area.

Whatever your favourite outdoor activity is, Seattle offers something for everyone. There's no lack of opportunities to explore and enjoy the great outdoors in Seattle, with its breathtaking landscape, rich animals, and year-round activities.

# CHAPTER 8: ARTS & ENTERTAINMENT

Seattle is well-known for its thriving arts and entertainment sector. Seattle is a cultural destination for anyone, with world-class museums and art galleries as well as a bustling live music scene.

**Museums:** The Seattle Art Museum is one of the city's most well-known institutions. This modern art museum has a large collection of current and historical artworks from many countries and periods. Pablo Picasso and Georgia O'Keeffe have both created notable masterpieces. Throughout the year, the museum also holds special exhibits and features an interactive family section.

Seattle is a cultural destination for everyone, from world-class museums to bustling music and comedy venues. Seattle offers something for everyone, whether you want to tour the city's art galleries and museums, see a concert, or just listen to live music.

Seattle is a dynamic city rich in culture and entertainment. This city provides something for everyone, including music, theatre, dance, virtual art, and literary art.

**Music:** is a common hobby in Seattle. The city is also known for its live music culture, featuring venues such as The Showbox, Crocodile, and Neumos. The Showbox is a historic music venue in downtown Seattle that showcases a diverse variety of events, from local indie bands to worldwide artists. Crocodile is yet another renowned venue that hosts a diverse range of live music, from punk to hip-hop. Finally, Neumos is a club that features a wide range of musical styles, from jazz to metal.The city is home to a variety of prominent venues, including The Showbox, The Crocodile, and Neumos, which accommodate both nationally recognized artists and local bands. Throughout the year, there are also various music festivals, such as Bumbershoot, that include a mix of local, national, and international acts.

**Theatre** is another prominent type of entertainment in Seattle. The city is home to numerous well-known theatre organisations, including the Seattle Opera Theatre, Intiman Theatre, and the renowned 5th Avenue Theatre. Throughout the year, these groups create a diverse range of plays, musicals, and other theatrical works. The 5th Avenue

Theatre, located in the centre of downtown Seattle, is a historic theatre that stages a range of productions ranging from musicals to classical concerts. The Seattle Opera is one of the country's leading opera companies, presenting a variety of opera performances throughout the year.

Seattle is well-known for its film industry, which includes a diverse array of independent theatres and film festivals. The Seattle International Film Festival is one of the world's major film festivals, showcasing nearly 400 films from across the globe. The SIFF Cinema Uptown and the SIFF Film Center are two of the city's most popular independent theatres, offering a wide range of art house, independent, and classic films.

**Dance** is a prominent type of entertainment in Seattle. The Pacific Northwest Ballet and Spectrum Dance Theater are two of the city's prominent dance organisations. Throughout the year, these organisations present a variety of classical and modern pieces.

**Virtual art** is another type of entertainment in Seattle. Technology has allowed artists to make art in the form of interactive digital experiences. These experiences may be found on websites, mobile applications, and even in virtual reality.

**Literary Art** is a prominent type of entertainment in Seattle. The city is home to a variety of well-known writers, publishers, and booksellers. From poetry readings and book clubs to author signings and literary events, there is no lack of ways to appreciate the written word in Seattle.

As a first-time visitor, you'll find plenty of ways to enjoy Seattle's entertainment scene. This bustling city has something for everyone, whether you prefer music, theatre, dancing, virtual art, or literary art.

# Nightlife in Seattle

The nightlife in Seattle is a bustling combination of music, cuisine, and alcohol. Seattle offers something for everyone, from throbbing dance clubs to dingy pubs. Late-night food, artisan drinks, rooftop lounges, and other amenities are available to both visitors and residents.

Whatever style of evening experience you want, Seattle offers something for everyone. You're sure to discover the right place to spend your night, from busy dance clubs to quiet pubs.Seattle's nightlife is regarded for being active and varied, having something for everyone. There is no lack of entertainment in the Emerald City, from music venues to pubs and lounges to comedy clubs.

**A. <u>Music Venues:</u>** Seattle's music venues vary from tiny, intimate bars to massive, open-air amphitheatres. With so many genres covered, music fans of all sorts may find something to their liking. The Showbox, The Crocodile, The Triple Door, Neumos, and Showbox SoDo are all popular venues. Each has its own distinct ambiance, featuring a diverse range of live music performances by both local and international bands.

Check out Seattle's Belltown district for a bustling environment. Some of the city's most popular bars may be found in Belltown, including The Crocodile and Knee High Stocking Co. The Crocodile features a fun environment with plenty of dancing. Knee High Stocking Co. delivers handmade drinks and small meals in a speakeasy-style setting

**B. <u>Bars and Lounges:</u>** For those searching for a more relaxing evening out, Seattle's bars and lounges provide a bustling scene. There is something for everyone, from dingy taverns and local pubs to expensive cocktail clubs and speakeasies. Tini Bigs Lounge, Knee High Stocking Co., Liberty Bar and Lounge, and Bar Ciudad are all popular hangouts.

There are lots of alternatives if you want a more relaxed evening. Some of the city's top bars may be found in West Seattle Junction, including The Skylark Café and Club and The Royal Room. The Skylark Café and Club features a cosy environment and innovative drinks. The Royal Room is a live music venue and bar that features jazz, blues, and other musical genres.

**C. Comedy Clubs:** Seattle also has a thriving comedy culture, with venues such as the Comedy Underground, Jet City Improv and Unexpected Productions. These comedy clubs host a wide range of stand-up, improv, and sketch comedy performers. Comedy clubs also provide a fun night out in Seattle. There are several comedic genres to select from, ranging from improv to stand-up. The Comedy Underground, Laughs Comedy Club, and The Parlor Live are all popular comedy clubs. A night of laughter and entertainment from some of the city's most skilled comedians awaits fans here.

Capitol Hill is the epicentre of Seattle's nightlife. The Cha Cha Lounge, Neumos, and Bar Sue are all popular bars and clubs. You may dance to indie rock, hip hop, and electronic music at the Cha Cha Lounge. Neumos is a live music venue that hosts concerts by both local and national artists. Bar Sue is a rustic dive bar that offers innovative specialty drinks.

# Tour activities

Welcome to Seattle! Seattle, home of the renowned Space Needle, is a dynamic city with a wide range of attractions and activities. Whether you want to take a leisurely walk around the city or go on an adrenaline-fueled adventure, Seattle has something for everyone. From excursions to experiences, these are some of the top things to do during your vacation.

**Seattle City Tours:** Take a guided tour of Seattle's various attractions. See the famous Space Needle, Pike Place Market, and more. The cost of a city tour ranges from $25 to $75 per participant, depending on the duration and kind of trip.

**Seattle Waterfront Tours:** Take a boat tour of Seattle's waterfront and experience its various attractions. Take in the views of the Seattle skyline, the Olympic Mountains, and more. Waterfront trips are approximately $35 per person.

**Seattle underworld Tours:** Get an inside peek at Seattle's secret underworld. Tours include a tour through subterranean corridors, tunnels, and more. The subterranean excursions cost $20 per person.

**Seattle culinary(local) Tours:** Take a guided culinary tour to sample some of Seattle's greatest cuisine. Explore the city's varied neighbourhoods and experience the flavours of the city. Food tours vary in price from $45 to $75 per person.

**Kayaking Tours:** Get out on the lake and see the beauty of Seattle from the seat of a kayak. Tour guides will take you to some of the top sites in the city and give a fun and instructive experience. Kayaking trips normally cost $50 per person.

**Helicopter Tours:** Take a helicopter tour to get a bird's eye perspective of Seattle. Fly over famous sites to gain a new perspective on the city. Helicopter trips typically cost roughly $200 per person.

**Free Tour:** There are several free Tour activities to do in Seattle. Explore the Seattle Art Museum, the Seattle Aquarium, or the Olympic Sculpture Park. All of these events are free to the public.

**Seattle Bike Tour:** Take a guided bike tour of Seattle's prominent locations, including Gas Works Park, the Fremont Troll, and more. The tour price is from $25-$60 depending on the location.

**Seattle Skyline Tour:** On a one-hour boat cruise, take a guided tour of Seattle's skyline and notable attractions. The fee cost $15 or more per person

**Museum of Pop Culture Admission:** Visit the Museum of Pop Culture to learn about music, cinema, and pop culture. The fee ranges from $17 to $31.

**Space Needle Admission:** The Space Needle is the most recognized landmark in Seattle.

The entry fee is $37 for adults and $30 for children aged 4 to 12.

**Seattle subterranean Tour:** This guided tour takes you under Pioneer Square's streets and into Seattle's ancient subterranean corridors. Adults pay $20, while children (7-12) pay $15.

**Seattle Great Wheel:** From the harbour, this giant Ferris wheel provides stunning vistas of Seattle. The fee is $14 for adults and $8 for children aged 4 to 12.

**Seattle Aquarium:** The Seattle Aquarium has exhibits, events, and activities centred on Pacific Northwest marine life. Adults pay $30.95, while children aged 4 to 12 pay $23.95.

**Chihuly Garden and Glass:** This interactive museum displays glass artist Dale Chihuly's work. Adults pay $26 and children (5-12) pay $20.

Seattle provides something for everyone, whether you want an adventure or a calm vacation. There is lots to do in this busy city, from excursions to free activities. Have a wonderful time!

# Festivals and Event

Seattle is a city of festivals and events, with activities for people of all ages. Seattle has something for everyone, from music festivals to art events, outdoor activities to cultural festivities.

The Seattle International Film Festival, the Bite of Seattle, and the Seattle Hempfest all take place during the summer months. These events, which offer music, film, cuisine, and art, are fantastic ways to learn about Seattle's culture and meet people from all over the globe. The Bite of Seattle is an excellent opportunity to experience the different cuisine of the city. The Seattle Hempfest is the world's biggest cannabis culture event, including speakers, music, art, and more.

Throughout the autumn, Seattle presents a variety of events and activities. Over 200 merchants offer local food, art, and crafts at the Seattle Night Market. The Seattle Art Fair is an excellent opportunity to learn about the city's vibrant art culture. The Seattle Marathon and Half Marathon attract thousands of runners for a day of competition and companionship throughout the city. The Seattle International

Beerfest is an excellent opportunity to taste artisan beers from all around the globe.

Seattle comes alive with festive spirit throughout the winter. Ice skating, tree lighting, and other activities are part of the Winterfest festival. The Seattle Great Wheel, which offers breathtaking views of the city, is a favourite destination for a romantic evening or a family adventure. The Chinese New Year celebration in Seattle is one of the city's largest and most popular events, including lion dancers, fireworks, and other attractions.

The spring months are full of events and activities. With traditional music and dance, the Seattle Cherry Blossom and Japanese Cultural Festival honours the city's Japanese roots. The Seattle Bike-a-thon is an excellent opportunity to explore the city on two wheels. The Northwest Folklife Festival promotes the Pacific Northwest's unique cultural history via music, crafts, and cuisine.
Seattle is a fantastic festival and event location, with something for everyone. Seattle offers it all, whether you're searching for a music festival, an art exhibit, or an outdoor activity.

# Sports & Recreation

Sports and leisure in Seattle provide a broad range of activities for both locals and tourists. Seattle is an excellent location to go active because of its temperate temperature and outdoor-oriented culture. From professional sports teams to outdoor activities in the mountains to public parks and beaches, Seattle offers something for everyone.

Overall, Seattle is a good location for sports and entertainment. With its pleasant temperature and plethora of outdoor activities, it's the ideal spot to be active and have fun.

## 1. Professional Teams

Professional sports enthusiasts may enjoy watching the Seattle Seahawks, Mariners, Sounders, and Storm, who all call Seattle home. Outdoor recreation activities abound in the nearby mountains, lakes, and woods for individuals who like being active. Hiking, backpacking, camping, skiing, snowboarding, mountain biking, and other activities are examples. There are also several city parks and beaches where outdoor activities like tennis, basketball, and soccer may be played.

## 2. Outdoor Recreation

Sports and recreational outdoor activities are excellent ways to be physically active and healthy while still having fun and appreciating nature. There are several things to select from, such as going for a jog, playing a pickup game of basketball, or going on a bike trip.

Sports and recreational outdoor activities may help keep you motivated and focused on your objectives if you want to remain active and healthy. These exercises may help you grow muscle and enhance your cardiovascular fitness. Outdoor activities may also be a terrific opportunity to interact and meet new people, which can lead to improved mental health and well-being.

Running, swimming, bicycling, tennis, golf, horse racing and hiking are some of the more popular sports and leisure activities. Running is an excellent approach to increase endurance and cardiovascular fitness, whilst swimming is an excellent way to increase strength and flexibility. Biking is a terrific way to travel about town and get a decent exercise at the same time. Tennis and golf are excellent for improving hand-eye coordination and precision.Hiking is a terrific opportunity to get some fresh air while exploring nature.

Golf, cycling, and horse racing are three of the most popular outdoor leisure sports in Seattle's world.

Whatever your fitness level or objectives are, there is a sport or leisure activity for you. With so many things to select from, you can find something you like while still being active and healthy. So, don't forget to enjoy the outdoors by getting out there and participating in some sports and recreational activities!

# CHAPTER 9: SHOPPING IN SEATTLE

Shopping in Seattle is an unforgettable experience. Seattle has something for everyone, with world-class shopping complexes, boutiques, and specialised businesses. Shoppers may buy a variety of unique things that can't be purchased anywhere else, from the diverse and bustling Pike Place Market to the sophisticated and posh South Lake Union area.

Whatever style of shopping experience you want, Seattle offers something for everyone. From the historic Pike Place Market to the sophisticated and posh South Lake Union area, customers may discover a range of one-of-a-kind things and experiences.

## Shopping Districts

Seattle's shopping sector is a swarm of activity. The region offers something for everyone, from high-end designer boutiques to small-town mom-and-pop shops. The streets are lined with a variety of stores and restaurants, and the neighbourhood has lately been revived with new buildings and restorations.

The University District is home to a number of vintage businesses, thrift shops, and independent boutiques that give consumers a wide range of one-of-a-kind things. Vintage apparel, furniture, and home décor may be found here.

The Capitol Hill district is home to a diverse range of shops, from record stores to vintage apparel businesses. There are also a number of independent booksellers, retail boutiques, and eateries, providing a diverse shopping experience.

The retail area is a wonderful spot to discover one-of-a-kind things and presents, as well as high-end luxury items. There are art galleries, antique shops, and unique boutiques offering anything from clothing to jewellery to books and much more. There are also several restaurants and bars that provide a range of food and beverages, making them ideal for a night out or a relaxed lunch.

The region is also home to some of Seattle's most renowned attractions, including the Seattle Center, the Space Needle, the Museum of Pop Culture, and the Chihuly Garden and

Glass. These attractions attract visitors from all over the globe, making the retail area a genuinely distinctive and fascinating location to visit.

The retail district is a great spot to spend a day, whether you're seeking a specific item or just want to explore the neighbourhood. The streets are often packed with people and visitors alike, and the mood is always energetic and thrilling. There's something for everyone in the retail area, and it's an experience you won't soon forget.

## Markets & Malls

Shopping in Seattle is a unique experience. There's something for everyone, from the renowned Pike Place Market to the lovely Public Market Center to the many malls and retail complexes.

Pike Place Market is the oldest continuously functioning farmer's market in the United States. It's a lively marketplace with hundreds of booths, each selling something different. Colourful flowers, fresh veggies, local seafood, and handcrafted crafts are among the offerings. There are other restaurants ranging from casual to upscale dining. The market also organises special events on occasion, such as live music, art displays, and food demos.

The Public Market Center is a smaller counterpart of Pike Place Market, yet it still has a lot to offer. You'll discover a selection of handcrafted crafts and souvenirs, as well as local goodies like chocolates, pastries, and coffee. The complex also has a selection of eateries ranging from casual to upscale dining.

For those searching for a more classic mall experience, Seattle has a variety of retail centres and malls. Bellevue Square, situated just outside of downtown Seattle, is a big, upmarket mall featuring all of the major department stores plus an excellent collection of designer boutiques and specialised businesses. There's also University Village, an open-air mall popular with college students and young professionals. The mall has a mix of chain retailers and independent boutiques, restaurants, and cafés.

South Lake Union is teeming with high-end fashion boutiques, art galleries, and specialised shops. Shoppers can discover a wide range of high-end brand labels as well as unique things from local designers. Home décor, children's apparel, and unusual presents are also available to shoppers.

Seattle also has a variety of tiny, local retail areas. From Capitol Hill to Ballard, each neighbourhood has a distinct mix of locally owned shops, restaurants, and cafés. These retail areas are excellent for obtaining one-of-a-kind presents, souvenirs, and other products.

What sort of shopping experience are you searching for? Seattle offers it. From crowded markets and malls to small local shopping areas, you're sure to find something to suit your tastes and budget.

## Outlet Shopping

Seattle outlet shopping is unlike anything else. Seattle provides a unique combination of urban sophistication and rural charm with its busy and energetic downtown. You'll discover lots of selections whether you're looking for designer clothing, luxury things, or daily necessities.

Tulalip, Washington, just north of Seattle, is home to the Seattle Premium Outlets. This outlet mall is the city's major shopping attraction, with over 120 retailers and eateries.

Designer labels include Kate Spade, Coach, Michael Kors, and Hugo Boss, as well as well-known retailers such as Gap, Adidas, Nike, and J. Crew. There are also a number of eateries in the mall, including the award-winning Tulalip Bay Seafood & Grill.

Northgate Mall offers a more personal shopping experience. This retail area is well-known for its fantastic range of high-end apparel shops, including Nordstrom, Neiman Marcus, and Saks Fifth Avenue. There are additional home décor businesses, jewellery stores, and even a movie theatre.

The U-Village is yet another fantastic outlet shopping destination in Seattle. This outdoor mall in the University District has an eclectic mix of retailers such as Anthropologie, Pottery Barn, and Williams-Sonoma. It is also the location of the country's first Apple Retail Store.

Alderwood Mall, Kirkland Village, and Eastgate are among the smaller outlet malls in Seattle. These malls provide a wide range of businesses and eateries and are ideal for finding one-of-a-kind things.
Whatever sort of shopping experience you're searching for, Seattle offers it. With such a

diverse range of outlet shops, you're sure to find something to suit your taste and budget. So come on out and discover all Seattle has to offer.

# Boutiques & Specialty Stores

Boutique and specialty shops are a growing kind of retail establishment. Boutiques and specialised shops, as opposed to standard big-box merchants, provide a more personalised shopping experience. They are usually smaller establishments with just one or two locations that specialise on a single product or service.

Boutiques and specialised boutiques, which cater to a certain clientele, are often situated in high-end retail areas. They often stock products not seen in bigger shops. This allows shoppers to locate one-of-a-kind and difficult-to-find things. Boutiques and specialised shops may also sell higher-priced brands or goods than typical stores, enabling shoppers to acquire luxury items.

Customer service is often emphasised in boutiques and specialty retailers. These establishments' employees are often quite educated about the things they offer and are eager to give individual advice. Many boutiques and speciality retailers provide extra services like gift wrapping, bespoke ordering, and customised shopping experiences.

Boutiques and specialty shops often have a distinct ambience that distinguishes them from other types of retailers. Many have appealing exhibits and décor, as well as a welcoming and relaxing ambiance. Customers are generally encouraged to remain and explore in this environment, making for a more pleasurable shopping experience.

Boutiques and specialty shops are excellent places to discover one-of-a-kind things and individualised attention. They provide clients with a delightful shopping experience as well as the opportunity to discover things that are not available anywhere else.

# Arts & Crafts

Seattle has some of the greatest arts and crafts shops anywhere. Whether you're seeking for resources to produce your own crafts or unique works of art, Seattle offers something for everyone.

For people who prefer making their own crafts, Seattle boasts some of the top craft shops in the country. From huge chains like Michaels and JoAnn Fabrics to smaller, more specialised businesses like Northwest Wools, Yarns, and Crafts, the city boasts a range of possibilities for people looking for tools to produce their own art. In addition to the conventional materials like yarn, fabric, and beads, companies like Northwest Wools provide unusual things like hand-dyed wools from local farms and spinning tools. There are also many shops that specialise in certain crafts, such as quilting and ceramics.

Seattle is a treasure mine of art galleries, stores, and studios for individuals looking for one-of-a-kind works of art. There is something for everyone, whether you want a painting, a sculpture, or a modest piece of jewellery. From the downtown galleries of Pioneer Square to the little mom-and-pop businesses of the Fremont District, art aficionados are likely to find something to their liking. The same is true for people looking for handcrafted crafts. Seattle has a thriving artisan scene, with numerous establishments selling handcrafted products ranging from jewellery and ceramics to apparel and home décor.

Whatever kind of art or craft you're searching for, Seattle is certain to have it. From materials to completed sculptures, the city is a terrific location to discover the ideal piece.

## Antiques & Vintage

Seattle is a fantastic place to go antique and vintage shopping. The city offers a bustling and diversified retail culture, with a large range of antique and vintage shops and businesses. From tiny individual shops to huge antique malls, Seattle provides something for everyone seeking for that one-of-a-kind item.

The Seattle Antique Market is an excellent location to begin. The market, which is located in the historic Georgetown area, has been in operation since 1982 and provides a broad selection of antiques and vintage things. Furniture, art, jewellery, and collectibles from all ages and styles are available. The market is open all year and holds yearly spring and autumn sales.

There are various businesses in Seattle that specialise in certain periods and types of antiques and vintage objects for people searching for more specialised products. The Seattle Vintage Mall is a good location to start. The shop has been open since 1998 and has antiques ranging from the Victorian period through the 1960s. The mall also includes an online shop where you may explore their collection without having to leave your house.

Another famous destination for antique and vintage shopping is Seattle's Antique Row. The row of antique and vintage boutiques is located in the Fremont area. Many of the businesses specialise in certain periods and styles, such as Art Deco, Mid-Century Modern, and Asian antiques.

The Fremont Vintage Mall is the place to go if you're searching for something a bit different. Clothing, accessories, furniture, and other vintage things from the 1950s through the 1980s are available at the shop. Throughout the year, the shop holds vintage fairs where you may discover even more interesting products.

Whatever sort of antiques and vintage objects you are searching for, you will undoubtedly discover something spectacular in Seattle. The city offers something for everyone, from little individual boutiques to big antique malls. So, if you're looking to do some antiquing, Seattle is a great place to start.

## Souvenirs

If you're searching for the ideal gift to remember your trip to Seattle, you won't be disappointed. Seattle offers something for everyone, from handcrafted products to traditional Seattle delicacies.

Begin your souvenir shopping in the well-known Pike Place Market. The market, which has been open since 1907, is teeming with sellers selling everything from fresh seafood to handcrafted crafts. Local jewellery, apparel, art, and antiques may be found there. There are also food vendors providing some of Seattle's most famous foods, such as baked salmon and clam chowder.

If you're seeking for more conventional mementos, the city's numerous souvenir stores provide lots of possibilities. These shops sell a broad range of Seattle-themed things such as mugs, magnets, and t-shirts. Many of these goods include Seattle's famed Space Needle, which is a must-see for visitors.

No vacation to Seattle is complete without a stop to one of the city's numerous artisan breweries. Souvenirs such as glasses, t-shirts, and even beer koozies are available. Growlers and beer bottle openers are available if you're searching for something a little more distinctive.

Check out one of the city's numerous independent stores for a genuinely one-of-a-kind keepsake. These businesses are brimming with one-of-a-kind products and handcrafted crafts that you won't find anywhere else. You'll discover everything you need to remember your vacation, from antique apparel to one-of-a-kind jewellery.

Whatever sort of memento you're searching for, you're certain to find it in Seattle. There's something for everyone, from classic goods to one-of-a-kind handcrafted creations.

# CHAPTER 10: DAY TRIPS FROM SEATTLE

When it comes to day excursions from Seattle, Washington, the choices are virtually limitless! Whether you want to explore the great outdoors, go on a historical trip, or go shopping and sightseeing in a neighbouring city, you're sure to find something to your liking.

The Cascade Mountains are a short drive away for individuals who want to experience the wonderful outdoors. Hike through the beautiful woodlands, go camping at one of the numerous campsites, or try your hand at fishing and other outdoor sports. The adjacent Olympic National Park is also a must-see, with stunning views of the surrounding mountains, woods, and rivers. For those who prefer to remain closer to home, Seattle is surrounded by numerous lush, green parks and trails, ideal for a day of hiking or bicycling.

If you want to go on a history tour, take a trip up to the adjacent city of Port Townsend. There, you may tour the historic downtown centre, see Fort Worden State Park and its landmark 19th-century military post, and take a boat excursion to adjacent Marrowstone Island. Other historical sites in the area include the Snohomish County Courthouse and the Cascade Tunnel, the longest railroad tunnel in the United States.

Visit the adjacent cities of Tacoma and Bellevue for shopping and tourist opportunities. Tacoma is home to the Tacoma Mall, one of the state's major retail malls, as well as the Tacoma Art Museum and the Washington State History Museum. Meanwhile, Bellevue has the affluent Bellevue Square retail complex and a number of other attractions, including the Bellevue Botanical Garden, Meydenbauer Bay Park, and the Bellevue Arts Museum.

Finally, go to the adjacent city of Everett for a day of water fun. Take a picturesque tour of Puget Sound by boat, or try kayaking or paddle boarding. You may also explore the coastal community of Mukilteo, where you can walk along the pier and take in views of the neighbouring Olympic Mountains.

Whatever sort of day excursion you're searching for, you're likely to find it near Seattle. You won't be disappointed whether you want to enjoy the great outdoors, go on a history trip, or go shopping and sightseeing.

# San Juan Islands

San Juan Islands day excursions from Seattle provide an exceptional experience. The San Juan Islands are an archipelago of picturesque islands located just off the coast of Washington that offers a range of activities for tourists. From kayaking and whale viewing to sampling the local cuisine, there is something for everyone.

Day visits to the San Juan Islands are a terrific opportunity to get away from the hustle and bustle of the city. The islands are home to a wide range of species, including bald eagles, seals, and sea lions. While exploring the islands, you may see whales, porpoises, and other marine creatures. There are several attractive sites to take in the views of the islands, including the San Juan National Historical Park and the San Juan Island National Wildlife Refuge.

Kayaking is one of the greatest methods to explore the San Juan Islands. There are several excursions and guided trips that provide a range of routes and obstacles, so you can choose something that matches your ability level. You may also hire your own kayaks and explore the islands on your own.

Whale watching is yet another popular pastime in the San Juan Islands. Thousands of orcas come to the islands every year, and you can take a boat excursion to see them. You could also see humpback whales, porpoises, and other marine creatures.

The islands also provide many opportunities to sample the native food. There are plenty of great alternatives available, ranging from seafood restaurants to farm-to-table diners. The islands also hold a number of festivals throughout the year, where you may experience live music, art, and local culture.

San Juan Islands day tours from Seattle are an excellent opportunity to discover the islands' natural beauty and culture. With so much to do and see, you'll have a wonderful vacation you won't soon forget.

## Olympic Peninsula

The Olympic Peninsula is a gorgeous, verdant location in Washington State's northwest tip. It has some of the most beautiful landscape and animal diversity in the Pacific Northwest. It is also an excellent day trip location from Seattle.

The Olympic Peninsula has mountainous coasts, old-growth forests, and an abundance of animals. Hiking, bicycling, kayaking, and whale viewing are all popular activities for nature enthusiasts. You may explore the various rivers and lakes, or enjoy a scenic drive along the shoreline.

The Olympic National Park is an excellent starting point for your day adventure. It is a must-see site with its beautiful vistas, gorgeous alpine meadows, and lush woodlands. Hike through the Hoh Rainforest, explore the Elwha River Valley, or drive through the park to see the animals. It has various possibilities for those searching for a more relaxed day vacation. Port Townsend, Sequim, and Port Angeles are all beautiful places to visit. Wander the streets, explore galleries, and discover unusual stores and eateries.

The adjacent Olympic National Forest is well worth a visit. There are miles of trails, campsites, and quiet lakes and rivers here. There are also several options for fishing, boating, and animal watching.

The Olympic Peninsula provides something for everyone, no matter what style of experience you seek. It is the ideal day excursion from Seattle due to its magnificent scenery, plentiful animals, and numerous activities.

# Cascade Mountains

Cascade Mountain Day Trips from Seattle are an incredible opportunity to explore the majesty and grandeur of Washington State's Cascade Mountain Range. The Cascade alpine Range stretches from Northern California to British Columbia and boasts some of the world's most beautiful alpine vistas. Cascade Mountain Day Trips from Seattle provide a unique chance to see the spectacular vistas of the Cascade Range while also learning about the range's distinctive fauna, vegetation, and geological marvels. They are normally one to two days long and may be tailored to the traveller's tastes. Hikes, snowshoeing, camping, and other outdoor activities are available depending on the trip. Tour guides are also on hand to give information and direction along the journey.

Cascade Mountain Day Trips from Seattle are an excellent opportunity to get away from the city and immerse yourself in the majesty of the

Cascade Range. You may discover the stunning alpine meadows, towering peaks, and crystal-clear lakes of the range, as well as the bright hues of the summer wildflowers. You may also explore the old woods and learn about the area's distinctive flora, animals, and geological structures.

Cascade Mountain Day Trips from Seattle also provide a unique chance to learn about the region's culture and history. Traditional Native American settlements, historic petroglyphs, and local history may all be explored. You may also learn about the Cascade Range's distinctive flora and fauna, as well as get an up-close look at the unusual species that inhabits this spectacular mountain range. The trip provides a memorable experience to visitors of all ages and abilities. Cascade Mountain Day Trips from Seattle will give you a memorable experience, whether you are seeking for a day of adventure, a quiet escape, or a chance to discover the culture and history of the area.

## Columbia River Gorge

The Columbia River Gorge Day Trip from Seattle will take you through the spectacular landscape of the Columbia River Gorge. Drive from Seattle to the Columbia River Gorge National Scenic Area, which runs from the Oregon border to the Cascade Mountains. You will be able to see the spectacular majesty of the Columbia River as it weaves its way through the gorge along the route.

When you arrive, you will have the chance to enjoy the area's various sights and activities. You may take a tour of the Columbia River Gorge, see the famous Bonneville Dam, or wander along the Waterfall Trail. There are also numerous historical places and monuments to visit, such as the Mark O. Hatfield Trail and the Lewis and Clark Trail.

You will be able to enjoy the natural splendour of the Columbia River Gorge, in addition to the sights and activities. Bald eagles, ospreys, and other animals will be seen. The river also offers opportunities for fishing, swimming, and boating. There are several restaurants and businesses along the route, so you will never be bored.

After soaking in all of the sights and sounds of the Columbia River Gorge, you'll return to Seattle with a renewed appreciation for the magnificence of this one-of-a-kind region of the globe.

# Mount Rainier National Park

Mount Rainier National Park is a stunningly gorgeous natural paradise situated only a short drive from Seattle. Visitors from all over the globe come to see the park's towering glacier-clad peak, rich old-growth forests, wildflower meadows, and beautiful vistas of alpine lakes. Mount Rainier National Park, with over 200 miles of trails and a diverse range of activities, has something for everyone.The Park has a lot to offer for visitors seeking for a day excursion from Seattle. The most popular day-trip destinations are Paradise and Sunrise, both of which are breathtakingly gorgeous and readily accessible. Paradise is situated near the park's southern end and provides spectacular views of the mountain as well as access to a variety of trails. Sunrise is situated at the park's eastern extremity and is the highest peak at 6,400 feet. Visitors may hike a number of paths and enjoy breathtaking views of the mountain and its glaciers.

Some of Mount Rainier National Park's top walks, including the Skyline Trail and the Cascade Loop, may be included in a day trip. The Skyline Trail, situated near Paradise, is a 7-mile round-trip climb that provides breathtaking views of the mountain and surrounding region. The Cascade circle is a three-mile circle through the park's old-growth woods and meadows.The Park also offers a number of additional activities to visitors. The park has a number of ranger-led walks that are an excellent opportunity to learn about the area's history and ecosystem. There are additional educational activities available, such as bird viewing, wildflower identification, and geology excursions. There are guided glacier excursions available for people interested in exploring the park's glaciers.

Mount Rainier National Park offers something for everyone, and a day trip from Seattle is the ideal way to see it all. Mount Rainier National Park offers something for everyone, whether you want a quiet day of sightseeing and nature hikes or an exciting day of glacier-hiking and discovery.

# CHAPTER 11: SEATTLE FOR FAMILIES

Seattle, Washington is an excellent destination for families. Seattle is likely to give a wonderful family trip with its gorgeous mountain vistas, different neighbourhoods, and plenty of activities and attractions. The city is plenty with notable sights to visit, from the Space Needle to Pike Place Market. Seattle also has a broad range of activities to meet the interests of any family. There is something for everyone, from the Woodland Park Zoo to the Seattle Aquarium and the Museum of Flight. Hiking, riding, and kayaking are just a few of the outdoor activities available in the city. It's also an excellent destination for families to spend quality time together. There are lots of exciting things for the kids to enjoy in Seattle, from the Seattle Children's Museum to the Seattle Great Wheel. The city also features a diverse range of restaurants and eateries, from informal cafés to upmarket restaurants, so everyone in the family will find something to like.

Overall, Seattle is a fantastic family getaway. With its distinct culture and plethora of activities and sights, it is certain to give an unforgettable experience.

# Family-friendly Activities

There are several family-friendly activities in Seattle. This dynamic city has something for everyone, from outdoor excursions to cultural encounters to creative pursuits.

Outdoor activities are an excellent opportunity for families to spend quality time together. Rain or shine, there are several opportunities to enjoy wildlife in Seattle. Take a boat to Bainbridge Island and see the tidal pools, or spend the day trekking through Olympic National Park's beautiful woodlands. Rent kayaks and paddle around Lake Union for a one-of-a-kind experience, or enjoy a leisurely walk along the shoreline in Seattle's gorgeous green areas.

Culture buffs may visit some of the city's most famous sites. Explore the historic Pike Place Market for unique goods from local merchants, or visit the landmark Space Needle for a breathtaking perspective of the city. The Seattle Art Museum and the Museum of Pop Culture both provide informative and engaging activities for the whole family.

There are several alternatives for creative pursuits. For a fun and instructive day, visit the Woodland Park Zoo or the Seattle Aquarium. Take a pottery lesson at one of the numerous workshops located across town. Kids may express themselves via painting workshops at the Seattle painting Museum or by participating in a local play performance.

## Aquariums & Zoos

Seattle is home to some of the world's most stunning aquariums and zoos. There are several opportunities for families to explore the beauty and wonder of nature in the city, from the Seattle Aquarium to the Woodland Park Zoo.

**The Seattle Aquarium**, situated in downtown Seattle, is an excellent destination for families. Kids will like the interactive displays, which range from beautiful sea otters to hypnotic jellyfish, as well as the touch pools, which allow them to get up close and personal with some of the aquatic critters. The aquarium also provides educational activities and animal encounters that are certain to please everyone.

Another fantastic choice for families in Seattle is the **Woodland Park Zoo**. This zoo is guaranteed to give hours of fun and education with over 300 types of animals, including tigers, bears, and even a sloth. A carousel, a petting zoo, and a bird sanctuary are among the other attractions in the zoo.

Another excellent choice for families is the **Seattle Zoo**. This zoo is home to a diverse range of animals, including African elephants and monkeys, and it provides educational programs and activities for people of all ages. The zoo also features a number of rides and attractions for children to enjoy, such as a small railway and a sky ride.

Families may visit the Point Defiance Zoo & Aquarium for a completely unique experience. This zoo and aquarium is situated in Tacoma, just outside of Seattle. The zoo has a wide range of animals, including polar bears, tigers, and even sharks. The aquarium has many displays, including a touch pool, a jellyfish exhibit, and a vast coral reef.

Whatever sort of experience families want, Seattle has plenty to offer. From the Seattle Aquarium to the Woodland Park Zoo, there are plenty of fun and instructive activities to keep the whole family entertained.

## Amusement Parks & Playgrounds

If you're searching for a family adventure in Seattle, go no further than the city's various amusement parks and zoos. Whether you want to experience the thrill of a roller coaster or get up close and personal with some of the city's most adored animals, Seattle provides a variety of alternatives for you and your family.

Let's begin with amusement parks. There are a few parks in Seattle that are guaranteed to please your family. The first is the Seattle Great Wheel, a 175-foot-tall Ferris wheel with a view of Elliott Bay. You may see the attractions of the city while flying far above it, creating a memorable experience. The wheel also features an outside observation deck where you can take photographs or just enjoy the vista. The Seattle Center, which has a number of rides and attractions, including the famed Space Needle, is another enjoyable alternative. You may ride a roller coaster, a carousel, or even a leisurely stroll on the monorail here.

For those searching for a more educational experience, Seattle boasts a couple excellent zoos. The Woodland Park Zoo is one of the greatest in the city, with species ranging from tigers to gorillas. It also has educational activities, such as animal lectures, where your family may learn more about the creatures they're seeing. The Seattle Aquarium is also a fun site to visit, with exhibits and activities like touch pools and informative presentations.

Seattle offers something for everyone, no matter what you and your family are searching for. Whether you want to experience the thrill of a roller coaster or learn about animals, Seattle offers it all. So come on out and tour the city to pick the best amusement park or zoo for your family.

## Theme Parks

Seattle's theme parks provide a multitude of entertainment, adventure, and fun for the whole family. There is something for everyone, from traditional amusement park rides to exhilarating roller coasters. The parks, which are located just outside of downtown Seattle, vary from large-scale theme parks to smaller attractions that appeal to a wide range of interests.

The famous Space Needle, which has become an iconic emblem of the city, is the most popular and well-known of the Seattle amusement parks. The Space Needle is almost 600 feet tall and provides a spectacular perspective of the downtown. Visitors may ride the elevator to the top of the tower and enjoy the breathtaking views. The Space Needle also has a SkyCity restaurant, a gift store, and interactive exhibitions.

Seattle Center and Wild Waves Theme Park are two more large-scale theme parks in the city. The iconic Seattle International Film Festival, as well as the popular Pacific Science Center, the Museum of Pop Culture, and the Seattle Repertory Theater, are all housed in Seattle Center. Wild Waves Theme Park is a traditional amusement park featuring roller coasters, water slides, and other attractions.

There are a few museums in Seattle that provide a more casual and instructive experience, such as the Museum of Flight and the Seattle Art Museum. The Museum of Flight has the world's biggest collection of vintage aeroplanes, while the Seattle Art Museum specialises on modern and contemporary art.

If you want a more classic theme park experience, Seattle has a few options, like the Seattle Great Wheel and the Seattle Aquarium. The Seattle Great Wheel is a ferris wheel that gives a spectacular perspective of the city skyline, while the Seattle Aquarium has both informative displays and exhilarating entertainment.

Whatever sort of entertainment experience you choose, Seattle has a wide range of theme parks to keep you engaged. So come visit Seattle's theme parks and build memories that will last a lifetime.

## Kid-friendly Restaurants

Seattle has a wide variety of kid-friendly eateries that appeal to families of all sizes. There are many places to eat with the entire family, from family-style Italian to basic American burgers. Some restaurants feature a play area or a particular kids' menu, but others have a more casual ambiance that encourages kids to be themselves.

Tavolàta is an Italian restaurant that caters to families. This quaint restaurant boasts an outside terrace and a play area for kids, as well as a unique kids' menu with typical Italian favourites like spaghetti and meatballs, macaroni and cheese, and pizza.

If you're looking for something a bit more informal, consider the Red Robin Gourmet Burgers and Brews. This renowned chain restaurant has multiple locations across Seattle and provides a pleasant ambiance with lots of games to keep the kids occupied. The menu has great burgers and sandwiches, as well as salads and sides.

If you like seafood, Ivar's Seafood Bar is a must-visit. This popular Seattle restaurant serves a broad variety of seafood meals for the entire family, as well as a kids' menu with classics like fish and chips, popcorn shrimp, and chicken fingers.

Try Lemon Grass Thai Cuisine for something a little different. This Thai restaurant boasts a friendly ambiance and a kids' menu with delectable foods including fried rice, noodles, and curries.

Whatever you're in the mood for, Seattle offers a plethora of kid-friendly eateries to pick from. From Italian to Thai, there's something for everyone in the family.

# Family Hotels

Welcome to the Family Hotel in Seattle, Washington! This hotel is ideal for any family visiting the Emerald City. They are located in the centre of downtown Seattle, just steps away from all of the sights and events that make this city a top destination. The hotel is created with families in mind, with large, comfortable rooms, handy facilities, and a helpful and kind staff.

Their roomy family-style rooms with two queen beds and a pull-out couch bed are ideal for families of any size. Every room also features a refrigerator and microwave, so you can have food and beverages on hand. Plus, our complimentary Wi-Fi and flat-screen TVs with cable will keep everyone amused.

The hotel also provides a number of facilities to make your stay more pleasurable. Swim in our outdoor pool, relax in our hot tub, and keep active in our fitness facility. You may also start your day well with our complimentary continental breakfast. They also have an attentive and pleasant team at Family Hotel which ensures that you enjoy the greatest possible experience. They can assist you with everything, from suggesting local activities to organising transportation. In addition, their on-site restaurant and bar make eating convenient, so you can have a fantastic dinner without ever leaving the hotel.

Make sure to visit the Family Hotel for a family-friendly stay in Seattle!

## Children's Museum

The Children's Museum in Seattle is an engaging and informative experience for children of all ages. The museum, which is located in the centre of Seattle, has various exhibits and activities that help children learn while having fun.

The museum has a range of interactive displays intended to help youngsters learn about the world around them. These exhibitions encompass themes such as science, art, music, and technology, and each one is intended to inspire youngsters to think and explore. Children may learn about the solar system, visit a life-sized copy of a rainforest, and take a virtual tour of the International Space Station. They may also investigate the workings of a radio station, make a model boat, or build a massive fortress.

In addition to interactive exhibits, the Children's Museum in Seattle provides a range of educational programs and activities. These exercises are intended to help youngsters improve their problem-solving and critical thinking abilities. There is something for everyone, from scientific experiments to creative projects. Throughout the year, the museum conducts unique events such as story time and live concerts.

The Children's Museum in Seattle is a fantastic location to explore and learn. This museum is guaranteed to give your children with a fascinating and informative experience
with its vast range of interactive displays and activities.

# CHAPTER 12: SAFETY IN SEATTLE

Seattle is one of America's most lively and picturesque cities. It has a lot to offer in terms of safety. The city is noted for having a low crime rate and is regarded as one of the safest in the United States. According to the FBI's 2020 Uniform Crime Reporting figures, Seattle has the lowest rate of violent crime per capita of any major American city. This places Seattle in the top five safest cities in the country.

The Seattle Police Department (SPD) is dedicated to ensuring the city's safety. They have a significant presence in the city and are active members of the community. Their primary mission is to ensure the safety and security of all inhabitants and visitors. They collaborate closely with local businesses, schools, and other groups to guarantee the safety and security of everyone.

Seattle has a lot of programs and efforts in place to assist keep the city secure, in addition to the police. The Seattle Neighborhood Safety Alliance promotes safety and security in local areas. Public safety seminars, safety walks, community gatherings, and other activities are examples of this.

The city also has a number of safety measures in place to keep residents and tourists safe. The Seattle Safe Place Program, which offers a safe refuge for victims of violence; the Seattle Safe Streets Program, which assists individuals in risky circumstances; and the Seattle Safe Parks Program, which provides residents and tourists with safe and secure parks.

Seattle is a safe and secure city in general. While there are always hazards and dangers, the city makes every effort to keep its citizens and tourists safe. Seattle is a fantastic area to live, work, and visit, thanks to the strong presence of the Seattle Police Department and the myriad safety measures in place.

## Crime and Scams

Seattle has a thriving economy, amazing natural beauty, and an active culture. Unfortunately, it is not immune to crime. In recent years, Seattle has experienced an upsurge in the amount of crimes and scams impacting the city's people.

Organised crime is a serious issue in Seattle, with gangs and criminal groups operating across the city. Drug trafficking, robbery, and extortion are all prevalent crimes connected with organised crime. In addition to regular street gangs, Seattle has a history of organised criminal organisations, including the notorious Seattle Waterfront Mob.

White-collar crime is another sort of crime impacting Seattle. White-collar crime is a wide word that incorporates a variety of illegal behaviours such as embezzlement, fraud, bribery, and identity theft. White-collar crime is often perpetrated by those in positions of trust and may result in severe financial loss for victims.

Scams are also becoming more common in Seattle. Scams are often performed by people or organisations that employ deceit to acquire money or property from victims. Scams that are common in Seattle include *online romance scams*, **pyramid schemes, and charity fraud**. Victims of these scams may lose substantial quantities of money or have their personal information taken.

In addition to typical crime, Seattle is home to a variety of cybercrimes. Cybercrime is the use of technology to perpetrate crime, such as hacking into computer systems or deploying harmful software to steal information. Seattle's cybercrime issue is expanding, and the city has experienced a rise in intrusions in recent years.

The City of Seattle is striving to fight crime and scams via a variety of efforts, including increased police presence, public awareness campaigns, and the formation of public-private partnerships to combat cybercrime. However, residents must be watchful and report any suspicious activities to the authorities.

## Accessibility For The Disabled

Seattle takes pride in being accessible to everybody. It provides a range of transportation choices, including buses, light rail, and ferries, to travel about the city and to major locations such as the Seattle Space Needle, Pike Place Market, and Seattle Center. The city also features an extensive bike and pedestrian network, making it simple to move about on foot.

Public transit in Seattle is simple to use and accessible to individuals of all ages and abilities. The buses are wheelchair accessible and include audio and visual announcements to alert travellers when their stop is approaching. The light rail system has accessible stations, elevators, and ramps to make it simpler for those with mobility impairments to enter and depart. The ferry system is also handicap accessible, with elevators to let people board the boat.

Seattle also has a number of accessible services and facilities to help persons with disabilities navigate the city. The Seattle Department of Transportation offers a free shuttle service for persons with disabilities as well as a taxi service for those who need help getting about. There are also a number of accessible parks, trails, and beaches that are meant to make it simpler for persons with disabilities to enjoy the outdoors.

Seattle also features a handful of accessible buildings with wheelchair access, elevators, and ramps. The Seattle Public Library has a large variety of books and resources that are accessible to individuals with disabilities. Furthermore, the city features a variety of accessible restaurants, shops, and other businesses that are meant to make it simpler for individuals with disabilities to move about.

Overall, Seattle is a city that is devoted to ensuring that everyone, regardless of handicap, has access to its numerous attractions and facilities. Whether it's utilising public transit, visiting accessible parks or businesses, or just enjoying the city, Seattle emphasises accessibility and inclusivity.

# Health and Emergencies

Seattle is a thriving city with an abundance of services to keep its residents healthy and safe. The city has a number of hospitals, clinics, and specialty medical care facilities, as well as a well-developed network of emergency services.

<u>Hospitals:</u>The city's hospitals are outfitted with cutting-edge equipment and manned by highly skilled experts. Harborview Medical Center and the University of Washington Medical Center are two of the city's most prestigious hospitals. Harborview is a Level I Trauma Center, which means it provides specialised treatment to those who have been seriously wounded or sick. The Seattle Cancer Care Alliance, the region's sole National Cancer Institute-designated Comprehensive Cancer Center, is housed at UW Medical Center.

<u>Clinics:</u> A number of clinics and healthcare professionals offer primary care throughout the city. There are two main health systems in Seattle: Swedish Health Services and

Providence Health & Services. Both systems provide a wide variety of services, including general care, women's health, mental health, and specialist care. Other clinics located across the city provide general care, mental health, and preventive care.

**Emergency:** To react to medical crises, the city has a large network of emergency services. The Seattle Fire Department responds to medical emergencies, fires, and hazardous materials incidents. The Seattle Police Department is in charge of law enforcement and emergency response.

Furthermore, the Seattle City government maintains a disaster Management Division in charge of disaster planning and response.
In addition to medical treatment and emergency services, the city offers a number of health and wellness initiatives. The Seattle Parks and Recreation Department provides a number of physical exercise courses and activities to assist residents in remaining active and healthy.
Programs and services to improve health and safety are available via the Seattle Public Library, Seattle Public Schools, and Seattle Public Health.

Seattle is a fantastic city in which to live, work, and play. Citizens in the Emerald City can keep healthy and safe thanks to a variety of resources and services.

# CHAPTER 13: WHERE TO FIND DEALS IN SEATTLE

Seattle is perfect for bargain seekers searching for the cheapest prices on everything from gadgets to clothing. Whether you're searching for something spectacular or simply a good price, Seattle offers lots of places to save money.

**The University District** is a great spot to get bargains in Seattle. This area is well-known for its abundance of vintage and thrift shops, which sell a broad range of products at inexpensive costs. Consignment shops, which are fantastic for discovering unique goods at reasonable costs, may also be found in the University District.

**Seattle's Fremont district** head here If you want to get a good price on gadgets. Many businesses in this region offer both new and old gadgets at low costs. You can get fantastic bargains on anything from computers and tablets to cameras and gaming equipment.

Head to **Seattle's Ballard district** for the greatest bargains on clothing. This neighbourhood is well-known for its clothes boutiques, which sell anything from designer names to thrift store bargains. You may also discover fantastic prices at the area's numerous outlet retailers.

Finally, don't miss out on the municipal events and promotions that take place throughout the year. Seattle features a variety of festivals and events with fantastic prices on anything from clothing to food and beverages. The city also has monthly flea markets and garage sales, giving you the ideal chance to get fantastic discounts on one-of-a-kind things.
Whatever you're searching for, Seattle is the ideal place for bargain seekers. You're sure to discover the right price with its varied range of retailers, events, and promotions.

## Discounts

Seattle is one of the most attractive cities in the United States, with a diverse range of activities and attractions. While seeing the city might be pricey, there are various methods to locate discounts and save money while enjoying all Seattle has to offer.

Using online discounts is one of the finest methods to save money in Seattle. Many famous attractions, such as the Space Needle, offer online discount tickets that may save you up to 20%. Signing up for email newsletters may also get you discounts on food, shopping, and lodging. In addition, some local Seattle companies provide discounts to guests who join up for their loyalty programs.

Another wonderful strategy to save money in Seattle is to visit free attractions. The city has numerous free museums, including the Seattle Art Museum and the Burke Museum of Natural History and Culture. Furthermore, many of Seattle's parks and beaches are open to the public.

If you want to save money on meals, Seattle offers numerous terrific alternatives. Many restaurants provide happy hour deals that might save you money on beverages and snacks. There are also various restaurant loyalty programs that provide discounts and incentives.

Seattle features various outlets and bargain retailers for shopping, such as the Seattle Premium Outlets and the Bellis Fair Mall.

Furthermore, several of the city's largest department shops, such as Nordstrom and Macy's, have regular specials and discounts.

Finally, if you're seeking hotel deals, Seattle offers numerous excellent selections. Many hotels offer early booking discounts, as well as discounts for AAA members and other loyalty programs. Additionally, there are various budget-friendly hotels and Airbnb alternatives that may save you money while still providing excellent lodgings.

## Coupons

If you want to save money on your shopping trips in Seattle, you're in luck! The city is full of fantastic sites to discover coupons, allowing you to obtain the greatest bargains on all of your favourite things.

One of the greatest locations to discover coupons in Seattle is at your local grocery shop. In their weekly circulars, most retailers provide weekly bargains and discounts as well as coupons. You may also join up with their loyalty club to get more discounts.

Another wonderful source to get coupons in Seattle is online. Many merchants provide online coupons that you may print and use in their shops. You may also locate discount codes online that you can use while making a purchase. Furthermore, there are several websites devoted to discovering the finest discounts in Seattle. These websites often provide special coupons and deals that you won't find anywhere else.

Coupons are also available in Seattle's newspapers and periodicals. Look for inserts and special deals in magazines such as The Seattle Times and Seattle Magazine. Furthermore, many local companies post coupons in their shop displays or on their websites.

Finally, don't forget to look for coupon booklets, which are often available at local businesses. These booklets may be filled with coupons for many shops and services.

With all of these amazing sites to locate coupons in Seattle, you're sure to save money on your next shopping trip. So don't forget to take advantage of all of the available discounts and promotions.

# Free Activities

Seattle is a vibrant city rich in culture, entertainment, and free activities. There is no shortage of free activities to do in the city, from exploring its many neighbourhoods to admiring its stunning natural surroundings.

Begin your journey at one of Seattle's many public parks. Whether it's a stroll through Olympic Sculpture Park, a hike in Discovery Park, or a picnic in Freeway Park, Seattle's parks provide something for everyone. Not to mention the Seattle Center! The Seattle Center, which contains the iconic Space Needle, is an excellent place to spend the day. Visit the International Fountain, the Museum of Pop Culture, and the outdoor amphitheatre for performances.

Do you like the arts? There are various free options for art lovers in Seattle. Every first Thursday of the month, the Seattle Art Museum is free, and the Frye Art Museum is always free. The Seattle Public Library is another great place to get free art and reading. There are quite a few galleries in town that provide free admission.

For music lovers, there is a wealth of free music in Seattle. You may attend one of the many local music festivals or the weekly concerts at the Seattle Center. Every summer, the city hosts the Capitol Hill Block Party, a free three-day music festival in the heart of Seattle. Don't forget about Sky Church's free summer concerts.

Finally, no trip to Seattle is complete until you experience the city's particular culture. Learn about the city's history and architecture by taking a free walking tour. To experience the freshest local items, go to local farmers markets. Or just wander the streets and discover the many neighbourhoods that make Seattle such a vibrant city.

There is no shortage of free things to do in Seattle, from parks and museums to music and culture. Whatever your interests are, you'll be able to discover something that piques your curiosity.

# CHAPTER 14:
# ADDITIONAL TIPS &
# RESOURCES

Seattle is a great city full of incredible sights and activities. There's so much to see and do in Seattle, from the famous Space Needle to the buzzing Pike Place Market. If you're searching for something a bit different, there are lots of other travel advice and resources to explore.

First, visit one of Seattle's many museums. From the Museum of Pop Culture to the Seattle Art Museum, there is something for everyone. The Seattle Aquarium is also a fantastic destination to spend the day.

Seattle boasts several parks and hiking routes for those who like the outdoors. The Washington Park Arboretum is a terrific site to learn about the city's trees and flora, while Discovery Park is a great area to go trekking. Don't miss the amazing views of the city from the top of the Space Needle.

Consider using the Seattle Monorail if you're searching for a different method to get about. This is a terrific method to go about town without being stranded in traffic.

Seattle has a plethora of lodging alternatives. There's something for everyone, from luxury hotels to budget-friendly Airbnb spots. Consider vacationing on a houseboat near Lake Union for a unique experience.

Finally, if you're searching for travel information, there are several websites and applications available to assist you plan your trip. The official tourist website of Seattle is an excellent place to start. There you may discover information on attractions, restaurants, events, and more. Travel websites such as TripAdvisor and Expedia also provide travel guides, maps, and other services.

Whatever kind of vacation you're planning, Seattle provides lots of helpful information and travel tools to help you make the most of your time there. With a little research, you can quickly locate the best locations to visit and activities to participate in.

# Website

## Hotels

1. Fairmont Olympic Hotel Seattle - https://www.fairmont.com/seattle/

2. Kimpton Hotel Monaco Seattle - https://www.monaco-seattle.com/

3. Hotel Theodore - https://www.hoteltheodore.com/

4. Hotel 1000 - https://www.hotel1000seattle.com/

5. The Edgewater - https://www.edgewaterhotel.com

6. The Paramount Hotel - https://www.paramounthotel.com/

7. Silver Cloud Hotel Seattle - Lake Union - https://www.silvercloud.com/seattle-lakeunion/

8. The Arctic Club Seattle - A DoubleTree by Hilton Hotel - https://www.arcticclubhotel.com/

9. The Inn at the Market - http://www.innatthemarket.com/

## Restaurants

1. The Pink Door: https://www.thepinkdoor.net/

2. Canlis: https://canlis.com/

3. The Whale Wins:
https://www.thewhalewins.com/

4. The Walrus and the Carpenter:
https://www.thewalrusbar.com/

5. Rockcreek Seafood & Spirits:
https://rockcreekseattle.com/

6. Lola:
https://tomdouglas.com/restaurants/lola/

7. Salty's on Alki:
https://www.saltys.com/

8. Serious Pie:
https://www.tomdouglas.com/restaurants/serious-pie/

9. Bateau:
https://www.tomdouglas.com/restaurants/bateau/

# Tour Companies

**1.** CityPass - https://www.citypass.com/seattle

**2.** Argosy Cruises - https://www.argosycruises.com/

**3.** Evergreen Escapes - https://www.evergreenescapes.com/

**5.** The Wild Side Tours - http://www.wildsidetours.com/

# Travel Resources

To help you make the most of your vacation, we've compiled a list of Seattle travel resources to assist you in planning your schedule and making your trip to Seattle one to remember.

**1.The Seattle Times** is an excellent source of local news and activities. It's a terrific way to keep up with what's going on in the city and learn about future events

**2.TripAdvisor**: TripAdvisor is an excellent resource for obtaining reviews and ratings for hotels, restaurants, activities, and other businesses. It is an excellent resource for learning about other tourists' experiences in Seattle.

**3. Airbnb:** Airbnb is a terrific method to locate unique Seattle apartments. It is an excellent way to find a place that is both affordable and offers a unique experience.

**4. Seattle Travel Blogs:** There are some excellent Seattle travel blogs that may help you plan your trip to Seattle. They often provide thorough information about sights, restaurants, and other amenities.

These Seattle travel sites might assist you in planning a memorable vacation to Seattle. These resources may help you make the most of your vacation, whether you're seeking information on sights, activities, lodging, or restaurants.

# CHAPTER 15: CONCLUSION

When it comes to travel, Seattle provides something for everyone. From nature enthusiasts to business tourists, Seattle can give a wonderful experience. Whether you're looking for a weekend getaway or an extended stay, Seattle is the right destination for a memorable and enjoyable vacation. With its stunning scenery, wonderful food, vibrant culture, and endless activities, Seattle has something for everyone.

Seattle has something for everyone, from the bustling downtown streets to the picturesque mountains. Whether you're here for business or pleasure, you'll find something to admire. Seattle is a terrific place to visit, from the famed Space Needle to the bustling Pike Place Market. With its diverse museums, well-known restaurants, and vibrant nightlife, Seattle is undoubtedly the right location for a memorable vacation.

Whether you're here for business or pleasure, Seattle will provide an unforgettable experience. With its breathtaking landscapes, wonderful food, vibrant culture, and many activities, Seattle is a fantastic destination for both locals and visitors. With its unique attractions, superb food, and active nightlife, Seattle is an excellent place to visit. So, while planning your next trip, keep Seattle in mind.

First-time visitors are sure to enjoy a fantastic experience taking in all Seattle has to offer. It is an excellent place for a memorable and delightful visit because of its gorgeous vistas, delicious cuisine, lively culture, and many activities. Whether you are looking for a weekend getaway or a longer stay, Seattle is the perfect destination for a memorable and enjoyable vacation.